The Consistent Overcomer

THE
CONSISTENT
OVERCOMER

FRANS M. J. BRANDT

WINEPRESS WP PUBLISHING

Printed in the United States of America.

Published by WinePress Publishing
PO Box 428, Enumclaw, WA 98022.

Please note: The contents of this book are not intended as a substitute for professional care and attention by a health professional. For example, it is always necessary to see a qualified physician before embarking on a new diet, exercise, or other physical health program. Any application of the discussions and/or recommendations in this book are at the reader's own discretion and sole responsibility.

Unless otherwise noted all scriptures are taken from the Holy Bible, New International Version, Copyright © 1973, 1978, 1984 by the International Bible Society. Used by permission of Zondervan Publishing House. The "NIV" and "New International Version" trademarks are registered in the United States Patent and Trademark Office by International Bible Society.

Cover illustration by Annette J. Blair, BFA, MA.

ISBN 1-57921-256-5
Library of Congress Catalog Card Number: 99-67062

To the memory of my parents—
Frans Brandt
and
Maria J. Brandt-Petschij

Him who overcomes
I will make a pillar in the temple of my God.
—Revelation 3:12

Acknowledgments

The responsibility for this book rests solely with me; however, it simply would not exist without the encouragement, help, and prayers of many individuals. I would like to express my gratitude to all who have directly or indirectly contributed to *The Consistent Overcomer.* These include Anne E. Bachle, JD; Judy Bailey, MSW; Thomas L. Bellinger, MD; Annette J. Blair, BFA, MA; Peter G. Brandt, BSc; Clayton J. Busha; Sue Davis; Patrick V. Demay, MA; Paul Gervais, Ph.D.; Nelson Good, MA, PsyS; Johanna C. Brandt-Kok; Ir. Jan Kok; James A. Leaf, BA; Kevin Lee, DO; Donald Mainprize, MA; Susan Mainprize, MA; Robert I. Matthews, Jr, MA; Andrea McCaslin; Kay F. Meyer, MS; Lloyd John Ogilvie, DD; Reyes Osuna, MSW; Paul Rajashekar, MD; Barbara Rondeau; Timothy Sleevi, MA; Helen Stone; the Rev. William L. Stone; the Rev. Frederick Sweet; Imagene Thomas, MA; the Rev. Herbert VanderLugt; Peter J. Vellenga, JD; Harriet VanReken; Stanley VanReken, BSc; the Rev. John Vriend; and, especially, Andrea C. MacVay, for her selfless dedication.

CONTENTS

Foreword   xiii
Preface   xv

PART ONE
The Determination of Overcomers

1. Overcomers Have Winning Attitudes   21
2. Overcomers Stay on Course   29

PART TWO
The Constructive Thinking of Overcomers

3. Overcomers Are Realistic Thinkers   43
4. Overcomers Are Rational Thinkers   47
5. Overcomers Are Positive Thinkers   53

PART THREE
The Emotional Well-Being of Overcomers

6. Overcomers Control Their Anger   61
7. Overcomers Manage Their Anxieties   77
8. Overcomers Defeat Their Depressions   95
9. Overcomers Lead Happier Lives   111

PART FOUR
The Discernment of Overcomers

10. Overcomers Are Alert Survivors in an Age of Folly   131
11. Overcomers Resist Follies of All Kinds   145

PART FIVE
The Perseverance of Overcomers

12. Overcomers Press On Toward Excellence   169

Endnotes   181
References   189
Subject Index   195

FOREWORD

The Consistent Overcomer is an exceptionally well-written and much needed book. It is a uniquely designed blueprint to help the reader make positive and lasting changes in his or her life. Dr. Brandt challenges the reader to rise above the mediocre and mundane. He convincingly describes what is required for true and lasting happiness, wellness and success, and then presents a well-integrated step-by-step program on how this can be done.

Dr. Brandt has succeeded in creating a very practical, and, at the same time, very inspiring guide to victorious living. He also sheds new light on why so many well-intended people fail in life. Winning in life, he correctly points out, requires a committed and stubborn willingness to live by truth, reason, and faith. There are no shortcuts to victory.

This excellent book contains several encouraging references to some well-known overcomers, but I also find Dr. Brandt's own personal story an exciting and inspiring highlight. The author is a living example of what it takes to overcome obstacles and to carve out a fulfilling and victorious life through the judicious application of faith and reason.

The Consistent Overcomer, filled with uplifting insights, is a dynamic book that gets right to the heart of the matter. Dr. Brandt in a clear and easy-to-understand style reveals how a person can live life to the full. He has masterfully interwoven the instructional with the inspirational. The end-result is a fine Christian book that will greatly affect the lives of many people. It will prove to be a lasting source of inspiration, comfort, and help.

RANDY L. CARLSON
President, Family Life Communications

PREFACE

Human beings, endowed by their Creator with faculties of reason and creative abilities, are indeed the "marvel of marvels." How wonderful it is to see them live courageously, even with personal handicaps and hardships of many kinds. How they inspire us when they heroically face famine, floods, or other disasters. How we stand in awe of their seemingly endless creativity, ingenuity, self-denial, or incredible perseverance!

It is marvelous to see them walk on the moon, travel faster than the speed of sound, reach into the depths of the oceans, and bravely explore outer space. Tenaciously they change deserts into fertile lands, wrestle virgin soil from reluctant seas, conquer devastating diseases, and create indescribably powerful sources of energy. It seems that no challenge is too great and no problem too difficult for human beings.

In other realms, too, we find those who are busy making history. Numerous individuals, for example, are learning to live healthier lives, master negative emotions, and reach out to others in selfless service. In the pursuit of excellence and a more sanctified life, they are fully committed to truth, reason, and faith, and almost always willing to get up one more time. With a sincere desire for optimal living they strive to become the very best they can be. These individuals are known as *overcomers*. All of them share one singularly outstanding characteristic: they have a winning attitude.

It has been known through the ages that attitudes set the course of our destiny and propel us through life; and more importantly, that most of us have a choice in this matter. Regrettably, all too many individuals have failed to discover or apply this insight. Overcomers, on the other hand, know that, broadly speaking, the way in which people think determines success or failure.

Thoughts, a major component in attitudes, are so powerful that they greatly affect our physical, mental, emotional, and even spiritual wellness. They can literally change the chemistry of our bloodstream for better or worse, and affect every cell in our body. Thoughts can even take on a life of their own. When strongly held and *consistently* practiced, they become beliefs, and eventually change into attitudes. These are virtually automatic reactions, which no longer require our conscious participation. In addition to a winning attitude, overcomers develop healthy personalities, which are marked by insight, openness, and flexibility. As we look at overcomers, we truly witness human excellence. However, our highest achievements are but a minor reflection of God's glory.

We so firmly believe in overcoming as a fundamental trait that we are dismayed to observe those individuals who succumb to negative forces of evil or circumstance. We are saddened by human tragedy and misery, and grieved as we observe the depths of human failure. Countless persons seem to find no joy at play, no happiness in their surroundings, no contentment at home with family or friends, and no meaning or purpose in their existence.

Scores of individuals fail to see the beauty of nature and are seemingly oblivious to the wonders of God's creation. They take good health and other blessings for granted. Countless men and women are being destroyed by the use of illegal drugs, tobacco, alcohol, and other aspects of destructive lifestyles. Many others suffer from mental, emotional, or physical problems that are the result of human greed, hostility, bitterness, hatred, and other curses of the unregenerated human mind. Millions of individuals suffer from self-induced depression, anxiety, or irrational anger. Others have a total disregard for the sanctity of life and live aimlessly from day-to-day without goals, hopes, or dreams.

We are also surrounded by individuals who have apparently become insensitive to the feelings and needs of others. Uncivil and devoid of a social conscience, we see them behave in crude, disrespectful, or tasteless ways. We can regularly observe sloppiness, laziness, mediocrity, and all kinds of uncivilized behavior in young and old alike. Drunkenness and gluttony are often considered normal. Self-seeking, self-serving, and self-centered individuals intent on pleasure-seeking and instant gratification sprout up like mushrooms. Many of them have personality disturbances marked by lack of insight, resistance to positive change, and uncooperative behaviors.

Why is there so much human tragedy, misery, and failure? As we observe the stark differences between human excellence and human wretchedness we are eager for an explanation. Perhaps there are two different kinds of human beings on earth? No, only one kind: the imperfect, sinful, fallible person. A closer look reveals that some fallible individuals are overcomers and others are not. In our search for answers we may also turn to history—only to discover that there is nothing new. Apparently, throughout recorded history, there have been those who have obeyed the lifesaving standards set by God, and those who have chosen not to.

Historically, those who have followed God's directives have done well. Clearly, these directives are designed to enhance life, not to bring destruction. Those who follow God's directives not only develop the healthy personality traits which are found in overcomers everywhere, but also such additional life-enhancing traits as *love, forgiveness, virtue, mercy, obedience, moderation, prayer, and patience.*

Some may think that genetic, educational, social, cultural, or economic conditions are the real reasons behind human excellence or human failure. Close scrutiny of history, and a patient observation of those around us, however, will prove otherwise. Vulnerability, we discover, plays only a secondary role. People fail or succeed primarily as a result of their attitudes. These, as we know, are subconscious all-powerful mental predispositions, which are the ultimate outcome of the habits of the heart.

Overcomers are individuals who focus wholeheartedly on mental, emotional, as well as spiritual maturity. They are not easily led astray or tossed about but seek to be fully attuned in mind and heart to the revealed will of God. They are not confused by clever impersonators of truth, or the many counterfeit philosophies that abound. They do not fall victim to ever-increasing temptations, easy answers, or the glib and glittering promises that are the hallmark of our present "age of folly."

Overcomers know all-too-well that true and lasting success in life is the reward of much toil. In this regard we need to remember the many individuals who are deeply hurting in a variety of ways: the sick, the hungry, the poor, the blind, the deaf, the paraplegic or quadriplegic, the oppressed, the persecuted, the abused children and adults, and so forth. Millions of individuals have suffered, or are suffering, incredible losses and hardships. Astonishingly, more often than not, it is among these individuals that we find so many overcomers. Why? The answer is that these are ordinary people who in spite of life's many trials have learned to think and act constructively, and have the courage and grace to get up one more time, every time.

May God bless you as you study and apply the concepts described in this book, and learn how to constructively deal with anger, anxiety, and depression; how to have a winning attitude; and, how to stand up against the many follies that seek to destroy us. You will learn how to have a victorious life!

FRANS M. J. BRANDT

Part One:

The Determination of Overcomers

1

OVERCOMERS HAVE WINNING ATTITUDES

Famous philosophers and poets, as well as religious leaders, have repeatedly stated that individuals are largely responsible for their own well-being, or the lack of it. Victory in life, they believe, does not depend so much on what, where, or who we are, but rather on how we think. This chapter briefly describes the importance of a winning attitude in the lives of some well-known overcomers.

Many individuals throughout history have discovered that being an overcomer is not so much an external as an internal matter. Abraham Lincoln, a man steeped in the wisdom of Scripture, once remarked: "Most folks are about as happy as they make up their minds to be." That statement highlights the active component of choice in our makeup. There is also a more mysterious element at work in becoming overcomers, one touched upon by the apostle Paul when he pleaded: ". . . be transformed by the renewing of your mind." (Rom. 12:2).

To many people it is self-evident that we are what we think, but perhaps the matter is not quite that simple. There are many individuals who think quite rationally, even positively, but still fail as human beings. The secret lies in the power of attitudes—those habitual responses that set the course of our destiny and propel us through life. An attitudinal state of mind is so powerful that an occasional change in thinking cannot have a lasting effect. For permanent success, we need a fundamental change of attitude. A renewed mind requires replacing self-defeating perceptions, words, thoughts, beliefs, and attitudes with life-enhancing ones.

The Power of Attitudes

Attitudes can be healers or slayers. They will determine success or failure, happiness or sadness, and often even wellness or sickness. Many individuals believe that human beings can alter the course of their lives by altering their attitudes—that happiness, wellness, and success are a matter of personal choice. This point of view is disputed by others, who stress, and rightly so, that people often have serious handicaps and great limitations. Many suffer from injustices and problems beyond their control. Others are victims of multiple negative experiences and hardships.

I agree that the world in which we live is imperfect. There is no absolute fairness, freedom, or justice. We live in a fallen and fallible world. Human beings also have different genetic backgrounds, training, education, experiences, and opportunities that may add to their difficulties. Yet, all of these factors have far less to do with victory or defeat than is commonly thought. The primary determinant for victory or defeat is found in attitudes. We can readily observe this in the lives of those who successfully overcame seemingly insurmountable obstacles, hardships, and limitations. Let us briefly consider the lives of some well-known overcomers.

Helen Keller—An Overcomer

One very famous overcomer is Helen Keller. She was born in 1880, and became blind and deaf at the tender age of nineteen months. Helen was a happy and healthy infant until illness struck a devastating blow. This illness deprived her of sound and sight and had an especially profound effect due to her very young age. Her mental faculties were completely undeveloped. How could she learn anything at all? Her environment consisted of only darkness and absolute silence; she could only grope around in an unknown world.

As Helen grew older, she became increasingly frustrated and rebellious. Her parents, however, continued to love her deeply and waited for a miracle. That miracle came in March 1887, three months before Helen's seventh birthday. Ann Sullivan, a teacher for the blind and an incredible overcomer in her own right, arrived at the Keller home. Shortly thereafter, Miss Sullivan revealed to Helen the wonders of God's creation. Within weeks Helen discovered that everything had a name. She learned to spell words with her fingers and was soon able to communicate with her teacher and others.

This, however, was only the beginning. Helen Keller would show the world, time and time again, that attitudes determine success or failure. She had absolute dedication and total perseverance. She not only mastered three different types of Braille, but, even more amazingly, also learned to write in longhand, neatly and legibly. On top of all of this, Helen learned to speak! Imagine a person who is blind and deaf since infancy, learning English, German, and French. How can a person who lives in a sightless and soundless world graduate from college? Helen Keller succeeded because of ambition, desire, persistence, practice, and more practice, which culminated in a winning attitude and victorious life. Helen Keller's life is one of monumental faith. She has become a great inspiration to individuals all over the world and her life is a powerful reminder that nothing is impossible with God.

Helen became a tireless worker for the deaf and the blind. Her books, speaking tours, and life inspired multiple millions of individuals to take a closer look at their beliefs and attitudes about so-called limitations and hardships. Even today, the example set by Helen Keller sounds a trumpet, heralding the good news—victory is possible for all who open their heart and mind to the promises of God: "Sing to the LORD a new song, for he has done marvelous things; his right hand and his holy arm have worked salvation for him" (Ps. 98:1).

Helen came from an orthodox Christian family. Helen, herself, however, struggled with various religious issues and embraced some views which are at odds with orthodox Christianity. And though these views will not be endorsed by many individuals (myself included), we cannot fault her incredible courage, hunger for truth and reason, life of faith, and great love for God and humanity. As a young girl she already understood the importance of love. In a letter to the Rt. Rev. Phillips Brooks she wrote: " 'Love is at the soul of everything. Whatever has not the power of loving must have a very dreary life indeed. . . . All the love that is in our hearts comes from him, as all the light which is in the flowers comes from the sun; and the more we love the more near we are to God and his love' "(Lash, 1974).

Corrie ten Boom—An Overcomer

Another inspiring example of a life of love is that of Corrie ten Boom (Carlson, 1983; Poley, 1993; Ten Boom, 1974, 1976). This extraordinary and courageous woman was born and raised in the country of my birth, The Netherlands. Corrie, her widowed father, and her sister Betsie lived in an old neighborhood in downtown Haarlem, a neighborhood I knew very well for I too lived there.

Corrie's father, Casper ten Boom, employed her in his watchmaker shop. His other children, Willem and Nollie, were both married. Mr. ten Boom and his two unmarried daughters were deeply involved in church and community activities, always reaching out to the poor and needy. They loved God and others, and lived in peace and tranquillity.

Their life of peace and tranquility came to an abrupt and sad ending with the shattering German invasion of Holland in 1940. Death, persecution and plunder quickly replaced safety, comfort and freedom. The Nazi invaders ruthlessly persecuted anyone who opposed them. Before long they pinpointed special target groups, particularly the Jewish. Many Dutch people came to the aid of those who were being persecuted. The Ten Boom family decided to help by hiding Jewish and other fugitives in their home. To provide assistance to those who were wanted by the Nazis was extremely dangerous. If caught, one would suffer a severe penalty. It meant certain imprisonment and possibly death. Yet, Casper ten Boom and his courageous daughters never hesitated to risk their lives.

A special hiding place had been prepared behind one of the walls of their house. If the house was ever searched, the fugitives were to hide in that secret place. The plan worked well until a traitor reported the Ten Boom family to the Nazis. This led to the arrest of Casper ten Boom and his children, as well as one grandson. The people in hiding, however, were never found and eventually escaped. After their arrest the entire family was taken to a local police station. The next day they were transferred to the much-feared German Secret State Police (GESTAPO) in Scheveningen, a small coastal town near The Hague. Later, the GESTAPO moved them to Scheveningen Prison. After ten days of imprisonment, Mr. ten Boom died. Eventually, his daughters, Corrie and Betsie, were sent to the Dutch Nazi concentration camp Vught, and from there to the notorious German concentration camp Ravensbrück. Here they endured endless brutalities. They lived on starvation diets, were exposed to the harsh elements, constantly humiliated, and forced to do hard labor. These God-fearing, middle-aged women, like so many others, were brutalized because of their love for God and others. The great miracle is that they never lost their faith or courage.

Corrie had been able to hide a small Bible, which she shared with her fellow prisoners. She brought faith, hope, and love to others, and by word and deed proclaimed the promise of God that: ". . . everyone born of God overcomes the world. This is the victory that has overcome the world, even our faith" (1 John 5:4). Corrie and Betsie continued with their habitual life-style: loving God and others through service.

What a contrast between good and evil. The cruel guards filled with bitterness and hatred, seemingly all-powerful, were the truly defeated ones, perhaps not only in this life, but also in the life to come. The seemingly powerless sisters, filled with the Holy Spirit, were truly free. They were victorious because they claimed the victory of Jesus Christ. They could say with the apostle Paul: "God did not give us the spirit of timidity, but of power, of love, and of self-discipline" (2 Tim. 1:7).

Although forced to live under the most deplorable conditions, they chose not to hate those responsible for their fate. Instead, they forgave and loved them. Corrie's sister soon became very ill. The concentration camp was taking its toll as she steadily grew weaker. After ten months of imprisonment Betsie died, but not before reminding Corrie not to hate those responsible for her death. Shortly after her sister's death, Corrie was miraculously released from the concentration camp. She found her way back to Holland and her hometown of Haarlem, where once again she helped those in need, being mindful of the admonition: "Carry each others burdens, and in this way you will fulfill the law of Christ" (Gal. 6:2).

Finally, the war was over. But Corrie, now a woman in her fifties, was far from content to rest on past achievements. She had become increasingly eager to share her experiences about the miraculous ways in which God had blessed her. She packed her bags and left The Netherlands. With only fifty dollars in her possession, she crossed the Atlantic Ocean bound for the United States of America.

More important than her lack of material resources was Corrie's undaunted faith in God. She had strong ambition, a clear vision, and great courage. She had an important message—one of hope and a future (Jer. 29:11), salvation and eternal life (John. 3:16), joy and gladness (1 Pet. 1:6–8). The world simply had to hear that ". . . nothing is impossible with God" (Luke. 1:37).

Corrie wanted the world to know that unfairness, persecution, imprisonment, or hardship are not the determinants of victory or defeat. Right attitudes help us to overcome life's trials and tribulations, and enable us to reach our longed-for destiny. Through lectures, books, and movies, Corrie ten Boom has touched the hearts of millions of individuals with God's message of hope and love.

Joni Eareckson-Tada—An Overcomer

Many others have had experiences similar to those of Helen Keller and Corrie ten Boom. Some are well-known, others less known, but certainly not less important. Among the well-known we find Joni Eareckson-Tada. As a young and talented girl she became the victim of a tragic diving accident. An athletic and popular teenager, full of energy and zest for life, she suddenly found herself completely paralyzed, a quadriplegic, unable to walk or to even feed herself. The only part of her body she could control was her head.

Joni soon learned to paint with her mouth and became an accomplished professional painter. If that was not challenging enough, she also became a writer, a singer, and starred in her own movies. We marvel at the incredible skills she has developed. She is realistic, rational, and optimistic. Clearly, Joni has a winning attitude.

Joni reminds me of the life or death offer that Moses made to the complaining tribes of Israel. Moses explained that the solution to their problems was not far away: "For this commandment which I command you this day is not too difficult for you, nor is it far off. It is not (a secret laid up) in heaven that you should say, Who shall go up for us to heaven and bring it to us, that we may hear and do it? Neither is it beyond the sea, that you should say, Who shall go over the sea for us and bring it to us, that we may hear and do it? But the word is very near to you, in your mouth and in your mind *and* in your heart, so that you can do it" (Deut. 30:11–14 AMP). If only more people would lay claim to the promises of God. Joni often struggled with her very serious handicap, but she was able to overcome her many limitations, setbacks, and problems. She learned to fully trust in God and to live by faith and reason. Joni moved from defeat to victory and became not only a successful painter, writer, and singer, but also an extremely competent spokesperson for the handicapped.

Overcomers are not superhuman beings. Like other human beings they experience discouragement and many other negative events which they have to deal with. But, by the grace of God, they manage to stay on course. In the next chapter I will share some of my own experiences which led me to firmly conclude that victory or defeat is a state of mind.

2

OVERCOMERS STAY ON COURSE

There are many dangers on the stormy seas of life. Overcomers not only manage to survive some of the most tempestuous storms, but also to stay on course. In this chapter I will explain why this is so, and how my own personal experiences taught me that indeed victory or defeat is a state of mind.

Overcomers, like everyone else, may get battered and tossed around. Those who lead a victorious life, however, look at problems differently than those who lead a defeatist life. Overcomers see problems as challenges, and difficulties as opportunities. During times of apparent failure, they still see the ultimate victory. They always get up one more time, every time. Disappointments and setbacks only nudge them onward, as if they are clearly seeing the hoped-for success.

Overcomers see troubles as a normal part of life. With Job, that righteous man who was troubled seemingly beyond endurance, they cry out that ". . . man is born to trouble as surely as sparks fly upward" (Job 5:7). Yet they have a predisposition—a mind-set—to stay on course. They may momentarily lose their bearings, but before long they are back on track. Like all successful sailors on the seas of life, they occasionally need to sail around obstacles, or patiently await favorable winds. They will remain steadfast.

They may experience the blackest darkness with stars and moon hidden from sight. Storms, too, may be very severe, and sails may come crashing down, but overcomers will gather strength once again as they raise the sails of faith and hope, fully trusting in the source of their strength—the One who said: "So do not fear, for I am with you; do not be dismayed, for I am your God." (Isa. 41:10).

Christian overcomers, looking to God for enablement and direction, safely reach their destination, as long as they face the storms of life with the compass of truth, rudder of faith and tiller of reason.[1]

Victory or Defeat is a State of Mind

During World War II, as a child living in the Netherlands, I regularly came face-to-face with matters of life and death—especially during the last year of that war when the so-called hunger-winter became so indelibly engraved in my memory.

The Dutch government in exile had ordered a national railway strike, and the Nazis did not take kindly to this latest act of defiance by the Dutch. As usual, the Nazi's took a number of punitive steps. They attempted to hunt down those who were on strike and haul them off to Germany, but most of the strikers went into hiding and escaped. Another drastic measure included the blockading of the city of Amsterdam, the city of my birth. This blockade proved successful in that it inflicted extraordinary hardships on the people. The extent of this disaster can only be grasped by those who witnessed these conditions.

Amsterdam, once heralded as the Venice of the North because of its many beautiful canals and splendid architecture, was no longer a city of life and light. There was no electricity, fuel or food. Every store was empty. Amsterdam had become a city of darkness, despair, gloom, and misery. Its inhabitants had already endured bombardments, curfews, cruelties and the arrest of many people, especially its Jews.[2] Everything, it seemed, had been done by the cruel occupiers to demoralize and degrade the defenseless population. Eventually the Germans plundered the city down to the last streetcar and vehicle. Not satisfied with stealing all forms of public transportation, they also confiscated all remaining forms of transportation, even bicycles. There was no end or limit to the plundering and pilfering. Radios were confiscated as were copper articles. Nothing was safe from the Nazis.

Bleak and empty shops, with bare shelves resembling skeletons, bore silent witness to the absolute poverty that pervaded the city of Amsterdam. A hushed, ghostly atmosphere prevailed. This stifling and oppressive state of affairs was exacerbated when the weather was bad, or when the darkness of early winter evenings engulfed the city. Every night the curfews and nighttime raids only added to the fearful knowledge that the population was being choked by starvation and oppression.

As the stranglehold on the city tightened, the population visibly decreased. During the days of the bleak hunger-winter of 1944, it was a common sight to see handcarts loaded with corpses being pushed through the city. Most of the victims had died of starvation or hunger-related illnesses. Those were incredibly pathetic scenes: broken-down handcarts being pushed by physically and mentally broken-down older men who seemed ready to be hauled off themselves.

The blockading of the city in 1944 heralded a new chapter of suffering for the people of Amsterdam. Living without freedom, food, fuel, clothing, or electricity had been hard enough. Closing the city from the outside world had more than a bad psychological effect. Many individuals, including children, regularly combed the country in search of food. I was one of those children. Meager and incredibly costly as the supplies were, they had given some relief to a few individuals, but with increased isolation it seemed all was lost. The people felt condemned to death. And condemned they were, for the Nazis wanted to inflict punishment; they wanted revenge.

People literally begged for food. Illness increased at an alarming rate, especially with such diseases as tuberculosis, dysentery, and hunger edema. More and more people began to look like walking skeletons. We wore old newspapers tucked under our shabby clothes in a desperate effort to stay warm. Furniture and books were systematically burned in our cement-block stove, which had been installed in our kitchen by a friendly elderly neighbor. During this time I was happy to have a pair of wooden soles for shoes.

Under these harsh conditions, some individuals lost courage. They gradually began to believe they had been beaten and developed a defeatist attitude. Many people were afraid to venture out of their houses, and certainly most obeyed the curfew that was imposed upon them. They became distrustful, anxious, and fearful. Virtually everyone had a friend, relative, or an acquaintance who had been deported, imprisoned, or had died of some hardship. Others cried from hunger. Many saw their young children die from starvation. Some were so ill they were bedridden. Few escaped the ravages of war and the cruel occupation.

No one could be blamed for becoming discouraged. Strangely, there were others who endured the same hardships yet never seemed to lose heart. My father was a true leader and a true overcomer. I cannot recall one single time when he was discouraged. If he was, he never communicated it to his family. He had a special talent for discovering something positive under the most deplorable conditions. A real overcomer, he always got up one more time, every time. My parents taught me by example that victory or defeat is a state of mind.

When the war broke out, my father, a reservist, did not hesitate to bear arms. I remember how he kissed us good-bye, standing extra tall in his green gold-embroidered uniform and round-top hat. I remember the tears and the sad farewells. I also remember how, only days later, he was safely back home again. The battle had lasted only five days, but much had happened in that short time. For my father and the rest of our family, the end of that short battle meant the beginning of a long and bitter war.

Since the country had been overrun, my father decided to give up his printing business rather than work for the Nazis or take the chance of going to a prisoner-of-war camp. He decided to pack up the family and live inconspicuously in the city of Haarlem, where he opened a bookshop in a quiet residential area. He considered this a safer place than Amsterdam. In 1943, however, we returned to Amsterdam and lived in another part of that large city.

When the call came for the imprisonment of those who served in the Dutch military, my father ignored it. Sometimes when he believed that things were too dangerous, he went into hiding. He repeatedly escaped the Germans. Eventually, he was tracked down and ordered to report for processing. My father would rather risk death than face slavery, so he ate tobacco leaves, knowing this would make him ill prior to processing. He nearly collapsed in front of the German physician who checked him out. He was so ill ("cause unknown") that he was declared useless even to the Nazis and sent home to die, but God healed and restored him and used him for service to others.

Another important event took place around this time involving my paternal grandparents. My grandfather, Herman Johan Hendrik Brandt, and his wife Johanna were peaceful, unassuming people; however, they were also determined, persevering, incredibly calm people, with a truly regal appearance. More important than their outward appearance was their attitude toward life. They had consummate faith. My grandmother enjoyed domestic things and was an avid reader. These gentle people were unlikely candidates to get involved in cloak-and-dagger activities, but involved they got.

They agreed to hide a young man who was wanted by the Nazis. As there was no room in their apartment for a secret wall, or empty hidden space, they developed a very straightforward plan. They thought that no one would suspect that an extra person was living with them. Their upstairs apartment had four rooms. A large bedroom used by my grandparents faced the street. There were two connecting rooms with a partition separating them, a living room and kitchen. My grandparents simply gave their bedroom to the young man and left everything undisturbed. The curtains were kept closed and the young man had the run of the apartment. Whenever someone visited (including relatives), my grandparents locked the young man in their bedroom. The plan worked well.

This young man, like many people in hiding, the so-called "onderduikers" (those who went underground), made some money by making handcrafted items. These were mainly miniature room interiors that were glued on a little board and used as wall decorations. All went well for many months until early one morning, for some unknown reason, the young man decided to leave the house for a short while. That particular morning there was a neighborhood *razzia* (a sudden roundup of people). The Germans would blockade a street from both ends, arrest all the men they could use, and transport them to Germany to work in the labor camps. The young man was soon caught and identified. The Nazis interrogated my grandparents, but they stuck to their story; they had merely rented a room to a young man, and they had every right to do so. The Nazis did not completely buy the story and confiscated all the property that was in the young man's room. My father's youngest brother, Johan, decided to demand the property back and amazingly succeeded in doing so. Sadly, after the war the young man never returned and was presumed to have died.

Throughout the war the pace and intensity of events never diminished in our family. The book business in Amsterdam brought my father into contact with people from all walks of life. This included people who would have a direct influence on my life—namely, the Dutch underground. It was not long before my father was supplying books to people in hiding. More than once I accompanied him on those dangerous missions. If a winning attitude was being formed in me, it must have been in those early years when my father discussed the dangers that could befall us. More importantly, he emphasized the hope that awaited those who were steadfast and trusted in God.

What a blessing it was to grow up with someone so oriented. His faith in God and country never waned. His sense of humor was always intact. He talked about the *overwinning* (victory) and never once about defeat. He talked victory, believed in it, saw it, and practically lived it. I, too, began to think that way. My father had a winning attitude; he was realistic, reasonable, and optimistic. He had a favorite hymn, *"Een Vaste Burcht is Onze God"* (A Mighty Fortress is Our God), and he knew exactly when to sing it.

He became increasingly involved in underground activities, supplying books and information, and passing out mimeographed newspapers. His courage was outstanding. When bombs fell he would calmly time the explosions and take us to the safest corner of the house.

One noteworthy Monday afternoon, a lone British Spitfire flew low over the rooftops of Amsterdam in search of a German target. In a most heroic solo performance, the pilot found the German target and strafed it with his machine guns. My father ignored the alarm calls and watched the attack, mesmerized undoubtedly by the welcome sight of the Spitfire. He would pay dearly, and nearly fatally, for his recklessness, for soon a machine gun bullet tore through his suit, and burned his clothes and chest before ricocheting off the cobblestones of Amstel Square. This event did not deter him. He ran after the bullet and brought it home in triumph, an ever-so-welcome trophy from Great Britain or perhaps as a memorial to the heroic pilot. Rather than stressing the dangers of this incident, it became a message of hope: soon we will be free![3] I still have the bullet.

One day my father called me to his side. He explained that life in the blockaded city was becoming intolerable and that things would get worse before they would get better. Unless the liberation came soon, many thousands more would die of starvation. He told me that he had made arrangements for my escape from Amsterdam. I was to go by barge to the province of Groningen in Northeast Holland. My chances for survival would most likely be assured, and the chances for survival of the rest of my family would be improved. There would be one less mouth to feed and one less person to worry about. I obediently heeded his decision.

Shortly thereafter, on what was probably the most miserable day of my life, my mother brought me to the main harbor behind the Central Railway Station. A seemingly empty barge, with black tar-covered wooden boards covering the length of the ship, lay idly along the wall between two piers. No one was in sight. Suddenly someone came out of the ship. After a hasty kiss and a hug, I found myself in the dark belly of the barge. I do not think Jonah could have felt more miserable when he entered the belly of the "whale." Jonah was only in that belly for three days and nights and had it all to himself. I was in the belly of that barge for many days and it was loaded with many young men, most of whom undoubtedly were wanted by the Germans. It was something I did not find out for sure, as a kind of standoff secrecy prevailed. I made no friends on that trip.

As soon as darkness fell, the barge slowly pulled away from the quay. The plan was to sail under protection of the night along the coastal waters of the Zuiderzee (Ijsselmeer). The first destination was Hoorn, then Enkhuizen, Sneek, and finally the city of Groningen. Here we would be picked up by Dutch farmers who would transport us by horse and wagon to Winschoten, a small town not far from the northern German border. On the barge we slept in hay, ate tulip bulb soup (those who could), and shared a large barrel hidden behind a few bales of straw for a common toilet.

Within hours of my departure I began to realize the impact of the whole adventure. I bitterly regretted having consented to leave. Sorrow and sadness for my family overwhelmed me, and I would have walked out of that boat and returned home if only I could have. I prayed earnestly for my family and for deliverance from my present predicament. God gave me peace and assurance that all would be well. I could echo Jonah's words, "In my distress I called to the LORD, and he answered me. From the depths of the grave I called for help, and you listened to my cry" (Jnh. 2:2).

We were not on a cruise and the boat was not a luxury liner. We were rarely allowed up on deck. Only occasionally one of the wooden boards was temporarily opened to let in a ray of light and some fresh air. The purpose was to look inconspicuous to friend and foe alike. We could just as easily be shot by allied fighters as by German ones. It was a frightful trip and a miracle that it succeeded. Finally, we arrived late one night at the city of Groningen. Farmers with covered wagons were awaiting our arrival.

I was too sick and too weak to stand up during much of the trip to Winschoten. I vaguely remember lying on the bare floor of a wagon with the feet of others resting on top of me. We were unloaded at a school building and taken to a large room where friendly and helpful women supplied us with warm food. However, I was too weak and sick to eat and found myself huddled in front of a huge potbellied stove. I felt even more miserable being exposed to the smell of food. I could not enjoy food while my family was starving. It was as if I had betrayed them. After all, it was I who had been most able to break through the blockade. I had demonstrated that by crawling through fields, crossing by rope over a frozen river, and sometimes being allowed to pass by a German sentry guarding the barbed-wire-barricaded roads in and out of the city.

I thought about the postcard I had written to my parents telling them everything was going fine. I even quoted Julius Caesar's "Veni, Vidi, Vici" (I came, I saw, I conquered), but I really did not feel much like a conqueror. I had given the card to a courier and many months later heard that it had safely reached its destination. I began to realize that I no longer had a family, a home, or possessions. I was sick and utterly exhausted; cut off from everyone and everything I had ever known. Not only did I feel separated from my loved ones, but strangely, even from the dangerous activities that had become a part of my young life.

In the meantime, my new home was an empty school building. My bed was a small section of the gym floor where heaps of straw had been piled, providing some warmth and comfort. After a day or so, I got on an open horse-drawn cart and was dropped off at the home of a woman who had indicated her willingness to take a refugee child. I arrived around noon and the woman asked me a few questions. She then gave me something to eat and told me that her husband would be home later in the day. There were two young children in the family and they seemed rather poor. My stay did not last long. It may have been a record in short-term foster care. Once the husband came home, an argument ensued between him and his wife. I gathered that the argument was about me. Suddenly, the man stopped arguing and turned to me. He told me to leave the house at once; I was evicted on the spot.

Mixed emotions went through my head as I tried to find my way over unknown roads, traversing an unknown town, to find the school which I had left earlier that day with such high expectations. My thoughts were sobering and my mood subdued as I rehearsed the events of that day. I found reinforcement for a lingering belief that it would have been better to be back in Amsterdam; better to be poor and hungry than to beg for a place to live.

Paradoxically, I also felt a sense of relief. If I was not good enough for that family, could it be that they were not good enough for me? Did God have something better in store? I did not know that yet, but I did discover that God was in control because I was suddenly in front of the school again. Yes, God was in charge. When I entered the gym area, I found that my corner was still unoccupied, awaiting its rightful owner. I was home again.

That evening as I was resting on the straw and thinking over the events of the day, my mood was still subdued. As I looked around, I noticed a young woman diagonally to my right, about twenty feet away. She opened what looked like a violin case. Could it be? Sure enough! Out came a violin and before I knew it, there was music—real, live music. The young woman was playing the Dutch national anthem, "Wilhelmus van Nassauwe." When she finished playing the national anthem, she packed up her violin and laid down to rest. I was thoroughly impressed and emotionally overwhelmed. Memories flashed by. I, too, had played the national anthem on my violin back home. I was thinking about the happy days at the *atelier* (workshop) of my Uncle, Geert Marree, who was a well-known sculptor and violin builder. It was he who had given me a violin and arranged for lessons with Louis Delacheaux, who came from Switzerland and was the first violinist of the Dutch Opera in Amsterdam. How much I missed my family and friends. I longed for the sweet sounds of the violins built and played by my Uncle Geert. Memories of the past came crashing down in a violent torrent, all clamoring for immediate attention; remember this and this, and don't forget that.

There were also thoughts of the present. How proud I was of that young girl. Here she was, a refugee in a strange environment, defiantly playing the forbidden national anthem. What an encouragement she was to me. As the soft, clear sounds of her violin vibrated through this large, cold and impersonal space, something marvelous happened. She had given dignity to the place, and more importantly, to the seemingly hapless mass of people huddled on the floor.

I had brooded far too long about my rejection by that poor man. My anxieties vanished by the second. I may have been rejected, but it did not matter. I was not defeated. I was not lost, nor was I forgotten. It was exactly as the Word of God tells us: "We are hard pressed on every side, but not crushed; perplexed, but not in despair; persecuted, but not abandoned; struck down, but not destroyed" (2 Cor. 4:8).

As the girl played, I was restored to full freshness and renewed strength, and I resolved to go out again the next day. I now thanked God for my rejection. I believed that greater blessings were in store for me; and they were, for the next morning I found the most wonderful Christian foster parents in the world. They received me with open arms. The prodigal son could not have felt more welcomed. My new foster mother ran out of the house, had compassion on me and loved me, as did all the other family members. I received the very best bedroom and everything I needed was abundantly supplied.

Many exciting events were to take place in Winschoten, but the most wonderful event of all was our liberation by Polish troops. I will never forget how I joined the soldiers as they entered the town of Winschoten—marching along with them as they shared with me some of their incredibly delicious chocolate. There I was, a young boy surrounded by hundreds of Polish troops in full battle gear who were in hot pursuit of the retreating Germans. It was one of the most exhilarating events of my life.

After the war I found my way back home, but soon was faced with yet another major challenge; I became seriously ill. For months I was confined to bed at home, until an ambulance transferred me to a hospital on the outskirts of Amsterdam. I was to stay there for over a year, yet being hospitalized became one of the richest blessings of my life. I had a great opportunity to read, think, pray, and reflect on the meaning and purpose of life.

This illness became a major turning point in my life. I learned that there *is* meaning in suffering as I discovered the importance of patience, perseverance, hope, faith, and above all else, of love. I learned that spirit is more than mind, and mind more than body. What joy can flood our soul even when darkness seems to prevail. What peace can come when we are stepping back from desired goals or projects. It is the very waiting and trusting in God that is so rewarding. This is very beautifully described in Isaiah, ". . . but those who hope in the LORD, will renew their strength. They will soar on wings like eagles; they will run and not grow weary, they will walk and not be faint" (Isa. 40:31).

I have mentioned a few events from my early life to emphasize that I have had ample opportunity to personally discover that victory or defeat is a state of mind. Most of my later-life experiences have reinforced and confirmed those early observations. I have had rather varied experiences which add to my conviction that it matters not who, what, and where we are, but that *victory in life depends primarily on how we think.* If our thinking is Christ-centered, we will definitely succeed (Phil. 4:10–20).

As a teenager, I left Holland and my family behind and settled in Canada; then at age 21, I came to the United States. The Korean War was still in progress and before long I found myself in the United States Air Force, serving my new country for many years, and gaining many valuable experiences. God also blessed me with opportunities to attend a number of excellent universities in both Europe and the United States.

My life and work experiences, as well as my academic and religious studies, have left me with the rock-solid conclusion that *victory or defeat in life is a state of mind.* The foundation for this state of mind is developed early in life. The good news is that even later in life—after gaining insight and experience—most people can choose to have the mind of their choice: "Do not conform any longer," cries the Apostle Paul, "to the pattern of this world, but be transformed by the renewing of your mind. Then you will be able to test and approve what God's will is—his good, pleasing and perfect will" (Rom. 12:2).

Part Two:

The Constructive Thinking of Overcomers

3

Overcomers Are Realistic Thinkers

Realistic thinking is factual thinking. It deals with things as they are and acknowledges that truth exists independently of our perceptions. Realistic thinking is synonymous with truthful thinking and the starting point of sound decision-making in every area of our life. Believers readily understand this, for they base their faith solidly on the Bible, which through the ages has proven to be what it purports to be: the word of God, which brings life and good news to all who listen to it. But, no matter how great our faith, we need to do certain realistic things in order to stay alive. This chapter explains how realistic thinking helps overcomers to enjoy more *truthful* lives.

Our Christian faith is reasonable and based on fact. We certainly do not check our brains at the church door when we receive Jesus Christ as Savior. Columbus undoubtedly had faith that he would reach land, but being realistic he also took along navigation instruments and food supplies. He sailed in accordance with the weather conditions, placed a lookout at the top of the ship's mast, and did whatever was realistically needed to sail west.

Jesus, the Son of God (God incarnate), walked on the face of the earth in a realistic and rational manner. He took time out to eat and rest. He prayed, planned, deliberated, and used wisdom in all of His dealings with others. He dealt with the circumstances as they existed at that time. He spoke the language of the people, obeyed their customs, and did everything based on truth. He exhibited self-control in His life, did not needlessly bring injury to Himself, and had definite goals to achieve. Jesus was in full control of His emotions, and never created unnecessary conflict with his environment.

Overcomers—individuals with winning attitudes who, in the pursuit of their wholesome goals, always get up one more time—must focus on facts. And as *Christian* overcomers they must focus on both the words and life of Jesus. Those individuals who pursue daydreams, whims, imaginations, hearsay, myths, or fantasy, will soon be defeated. Overcomers, however, know that there are realistic laws for happiness, wellness, and success. Happiness, for example, requires factual perceptions, pleasant words and thoughts, and obedience to the laws of God.

There are those who believe that with faith we can do anything we want. That kind of thinking, however, is usually taken out of context. Truth and reason must precede faith: ". . . faith comes from hearing the message, and the message is heard through the word of Christ" (Rom. 10:17). And this obviously makes very good sense. After all, are we able to understand complex mathematical equations, or solve intricate problems in physics by faith without training in the subject? The answer is *no,* unless we are talking about a miracle, which is the exception and not the rule. We cannot find the right solution to mathematical problems unless we have studied mathematics, and we don't translate a book into a foreign language unless we have thoroughly studied that language. While faith is essential for success in life, factual information, as a rule, is still a prerequisite. It makes no difference whether we are speaking about mental, emotional, or spiritual matters—only the truth will set us free.

Realistic Thinking Is Truthful

To get along with others, as well as ourselves, we must understand that *all* human beings are fallible. According to the Bible all people are sinners, come short of God's glory and righteousness, and are in need of redemption. Our fallibility and imperfection can be seen in most things we do. Overcomers fully accept the fact that all human beings are fallible, yet hold themselves responsible for their own happiness, wellness, or success, regardless of limited choices or vulnerability. They readily agree with D. L. Moody who said: "I have never met a man who has given me as much trouble as myself" (Montapert, 1964). Only committed and responsible individuals can be overcomers. These are people who do things wholeheartedly—with body, mind, and spirit. Overcomers are insightful and accept full responsibility for their thoughts, feelings, and actions.

Overcomers are scrupulously honest, not only with others, but also with themselves. For example, they only persevere as long as it is morally and intelligently warranted. They do not go against objective reality, unlike some individuals who are engaged in disastrous ventures, yet convince themselves that things are all right and persist until the bitter end, with the result being bankruptcy, loss of health, or loss of loved ones. Some may even claim to be overcomers, but they are not. Overcomers persevere in the pursuit of only *wholesome* goals. These goals must be honest, factual, and conducive to our well-being, and the well-being of others.

Because realistic thinking is synonymous with truth, it is rather obvious that Christian believers are to be passionately committed to it. Standing before Pontius Pilate, Jesus told him ". . . I came into the world, to testify to the truth. Everyone on the side of truth listens to me." And then, in response to that proclamation, the Roman ruler asked the well-known question, "What is truth?" (John 18:37,38). That question is one that has been asked through the ages by scholars and philosophers alike. In our modern and all-too-corrupt society, the question of truth has regrettably taken an altogether new meaning. Truth is seen as a subjective matter. "Everything," many individuals now claim, "is relative. Truth depends on one's point of view." As Christians, however, we know that truth exists independently of our perceptions, thoughts, and beliefs. Truth is based on fact, not fiction; on objective reality, not fanciful feelings.

Truth stands in opposition to falsehood; truth speaks of the nature and reality of things as they are, not on how we might like them or believe them to be. Of course, as human beings we are, and we remain, fallible and imperfect. The latter, however, makes us all the more desirous of truth. Whenever we speak, we speak in accordance with the persuasions of our mind—a mind that is filled with both objective and subjective information. It is our duty to seek Godly discernment, and by the power of the Holy Spirit live truthful lives. As Christians we know that the kingdom of God is a spiritual kingdom founded on truth. The more realistic our thinking, the greater and deeper will be our appreciation of God's eternal truth. Whatever decisions we make, they must be in line with objective reality, starting with the Word of God. Realistic thinkers know, however, that as fallible and imperfect creatures they can only approximate objective reality. No wonder that throughout the Scriptures we find so much emphasis on the truth—truth based on everlasting reality; on eternal facts, rather than subjective assumptions.[1]

4

OVERCOMERS ARE
RATIONAL THINKERS

Rational thinking is synonymous with reason. It is analytical, appropriate, explanatory, objective, and logical, and ensures the validity and reliability of our thoughts. This chapter explains how reason helps overcomers to enjoy more *balanced* lives.

Realistic thinking, as discussed in the previous chapter, is mainly concerned with identifying truth. Rational thinking, on the other hand, is primarily concerned with processing truth. Consequently, rational thinking does not necessarily accept all events as they are presented, but may take a closer look by challenging their reliability (authenticity and credibility), and validity (relative effectiveness). What may seem factual is not always so. Our mind (brain) is the primary problem here. The mind acts as an imperfect camera—one that is hindered by biases, prejudices, fears, hopes, and dreams. There are also other limitations, for example those imposed by different levels of functioning of the left and right hemispheres of the brain. Overcomers, however, frequently challenge their perceptions, thoughts, and feelings—they seek verification, even for some things that might at first appear rather obvious.

The ability and willingness to make rational decisions is essential for a happy, healthy, and successful life. Rational thinking assists us in finding the truth and then using it successfully. How can we start doing this? The first step is to actively resist the folly of impulse and to hold on to reason, even if it appears less attractive at times. Most of the immorality, crime, violence, delinquencies, and multiple other sins and worrisome events are due to impulsive stupidity or pervasive ignorance.

And many of our emotional problems—ranging from dysfunctional anger, anxiety, and depression, to disabling fear and worry—are often the final outcome of unchallenged erroneous perceptions and faulty self-talk. Unless we embrace rational thinking we will needlessly suffer from many self-defeating beliefs and attitudes. Rational thinking helps us to make sound decisions, especially if we make sure that it is life-enhancing, goal-achieving, and helps us get along with others. Let's have a look at this.

Rational Thinking is Life-Enhancing

Overcomers desire to stay alive as long and as happily as possible. They have a great respect for life and they do not waste it. Certainly there is little value in being successful in one's personal, business, or social life if one is unable to enjoy its benefits. Life is not only precious, it is also preciously short—at least here on earth. Human beings are creatures of the moment. Boris Pasternak, the famous Russian poet, vividly portrays the brevity of life in *Dr. Zhivago* when he cries out, "Life is only an instant, only the dissolving of ourselves in the selves of all others." Believers have learned from the prayer of Moses to count their days so that they may gain a heart of wisdom (Ps. 90:12).

That wisdom, however, is in short supply in our culture. About 85 percent of physical and mental/emotional illness is caused by self-defeating lifestyles. Obviously, most individuals do not apply rational thinking in their lives. All-too-often they search for escape in the so-called "good life," and, sadly, may get involved with drug abuse and other sins of dissipation. Victory and a truly joyful life, on the other hand, is found in obedience, gratitude, humility, service, faith, hope, and love.

Any action that is life-destroying is irrational. All-too-many people are addicts—slaves to alcohol, drugs, or other harmful substances. As they increasingly poison their bodies and minds, they are increasingly unable to make rational decisions. Rational thinkers, however, do whatever is necessary to live as long and as happily as possible. They abstain from anything that is life-destroying. They usually participate in regular exercise, maintain their weight at a reasonable level, get a sufficient amount of sleep, and develop healthy eating habits. Overcomers know that life is precious and do their very best to do those things that are life-enhancing.[1]

Rational Thinking is Goal Achieving

Overcomers reach their goals by clearly defining them. Some not only set goals, but picture themselves as having already achieved them. Even as they work toward their goals, they enjoy seeing the final outcome. Success in life is more readily attained if we know what we want.

Overcomers look for opportunities to discover, explore, learn, and grow—for they know that inactivity spells defeat. Goal-setting and happiness go hand-in-hand. As Helen Keller said, "Many people have a wrong idea about what constitutes happiness. It is not attained through self-gratification, but through fidelity to a worthy purpose." A sense of personal worth depends greatly on goal-achievement. Without goal-achievement the chance for happiness is seriously diminished. Overcomers have well-defined goals which they reevaluate regularly. Certainly the main goal for Christian overcomers is to have spiritual maturity (cf. 1 Cor. 13; 2 Cor. 8: 1–5; and 2 Pet. 1:4).

Most people want to feel calm, happy, and at peace with themselves and their environment, yet relatively few reach this potential goal. Too many individuals simply expect others to make them happy. They have failed to discover that every person creates his or her own feelings—good or bad. While the environment may provide circumstances and conditions to which we respond, we remain the only ones who can choose our responses.

Overcomers understand that negative thoughts bring negative feelings, and that positive thoughts lead to positive feelings. The secret of feeling happy or unhappy is found in how we respond to our perceptions of facts and events because that is how our brain works—we think with the so-called thinking portion of our brain (the neocortex) which, in turn, relays information to the feeling portion of our brain (the limbic system). Good feelings always follow good thinking. We are in control of our feelings as long as we are in control of our thinking.

Rational Thinking Helps Us to Get Along With Others

We live in a hostile world, filled with conflict. Every day thousands of people die or are maimed in wars that are going on in various parts of the world. We sometimes hear that we are enjoying the longest period of peace. This, however, only pertains to global warfare, since *every day* there is a regional war going on somewhere. Multiple millions of individuals have been killed since World War II. Actually millions of individuals are being killed every year!

Every day there is some kind of violent or nonviolent conflict in every hamlet, village and city of this country, and indeed the world. There is also some form of conflict in every home, every relationship, and even within every human being. It is important to recognize that, in whatever form, the powers of darkness are seeking to destroy human happiness. Ultimately every type of conflict is a conflict between the forces of good and evil, between light and darkness (Eph. 6:12).

How are we to hold our own under these circumstances? The Bible says by practicing truth, integrity, moral rectitude, right standing with God, faith, salvation, the Word of God, and prayer (Eph. 6:13–18). These are life-enhancing choices.

Overcomers know that much conflict can be reduced by understanding human behavior. For example, they understand that every person believes himself or herself to be right in his or her own eyes (Prov. 21:2), while in actuality every person perceives and experiences things differently. If we more fully accept our human fallibility it will be easier to get along with one another.

We must seek to prevent all unnecessary conflict. Happily, overcomers have less conflict with others. They quickly apologize, admit their mistakes, and ask for forgiveness. Overcomers seek to reduce conflict whenever this is ethically possible; but they also assert themselves, speak the truth, defend their beliefs, and live their lives without fear or worry.

To a great extent overcomers are successful because of their willingness to reason with themselves and with others. Rational thinking also provides the necessary balance between realistic and positive thinking. For example, those who live only by realistic thinking may not get anywhere if they are afraid to take any risks. On the other hand, those who are overly optimistic might violate the laws of God and nature, and fail in attempt after attempt to succeed in life. Reason balances realism and optimism. Rational thinking ultimately is solution-focused; it is based on objective reality and logic—the kind of thinking that ensures our long-term survival. This is what I have said elsewhere:

> Right thinking—thinking rooted in God's perspective on human life—is oriented to truth. It does not wish to wear blinders. It is open to the reality, which heals body, mind, and spirit. The ultimate in right thinking is to think as God thinks. "Let this mind be in you, which was also in Christ Jesus" (Phil. 2:5). Christ did not stand upon his privileges, but as the Bible vividly puts it, ". . . took the form of a servant . . ." (Phil. 2:7). This is the model for right thinking. (Brandt, 1988).

In summary, rational thinking is marked by a desire for scrupulous honesty, accountability, and responsibility. It emphasizes the need to evaluate, and, if necessary, to update our thoughts, feelings, and actions. The key word is choice, the challenge is honesty, and the objective is to do the best we can do!

5

OVERCOMERS ARE POSITIVE THINKERS

Positive thinking is closely related to faith. It is confident and constructive, rather than doubtful and destructive, qualities characteristic of negative thinking. This chapter explains how both positive thinking and faith help overcomers to enjoy more *hopeful* lives.

P ositive thinking is related to faith, but it is not at all identical to it. Faith, as I have explained in *The Renewed Mind*, is a gift from God, but positive thinking is only a learned mental ability—an acquired skill—a skill that is very important, however, for a happy, healthy, and successful life. One of the more obvious fruits of positive thinking is cheerfulness. The latter is not only helpful in dealing with everyday challenges, but is an important element for good mental, emotional, and physical health.

Overcomers are, generally speaking, happy, outgoing, good-natured, and spirited individuals. They have a free-and-easy air about them. They are friendly to others and readily share their resources. Proverbs (15:13) tells us that: "A happy heart makes the face cheerful. . . ." Overcomers readily smile and laugh. Their cheerfulness is both contagious and self-reinforcing, as it makes them feel better about themselves, and more attractive to others. Cheerfulness is, of course, the logical outcome of cheerful thoughts, and for this we need cheerful words. I remember part of a little poem, by an author who is unknown to me, which beautifully highlights the power of words:

> A careless word may kindle strife
> A cruel word may wreck a life
> A timely word may lessen stress
> A loving word may heal and bless.

The author of this lovely poem is, of course, completely correct. We must speak right if we are to feel right: "A man finds joy in giving an apt reply—and how good is a timely word" (Prov.15:23). Among the more noticeable benefits of cheerfulness are increased levels of energy and fitness. There is a direct relationship between cheerfulness and health. Scientists, for example, have discovered that laughing and smiling can have a positive influence on our immune systems. Since most of our illnesses are stress related we may want to pay heed. Serious illness, it seems, can be aggravated or caused by excessive anger, depression, and worry. Cheerfulness is a wonderful medicine for body and mind, while pessimism is a terrible poison: "A cheerful heart is good medicine, but a crushed spirit dries up the bones" (Prov. 17:22).

Positive Thinking is Confident

Overcomers look to the future with great anticipation. They expect that good things will happen: "For I know the thoughts *and* plans that I have for you, says the Lord, thoughts *and* plans for welfare *and* peace, and not for evil, to give you hope in your final outcome" (Jer. 29:11 AMP). Overcomers understand that faith calls for initiation, action and commitment. Overcomers do not hope for just anything that may come their way, but rather for very specific things.

Overcomers are people like the Wright brothers, who persevered until they finally got their flying machine into the air; Thomas Edison, who provided the world with the first electric light bulb; and Alexander Graham Bell, who gave us the telephone and telegraph. Of course, no amount of confidence would have created one airplane, one light bulb, or one telephone. Every noteworthy human accomplishment is based on realistic, rational, *and* positive thinking. Christians are confident because they believe that everything is always ordered for the best, that God is in charge, and that the future is bright.

With confidence and faith some of the most incredible things happen. A number of years ago I was traveling, via Amsterdam, Holland, to Great Britain where I was to present a three-day seminar. I had purchased a ticket on standby to fly from Amsterdam to London, England. It was very crowded in the boarding area where I was waiting to be called. Somehow, prior to my boarding the plane, I had lost my passport, but when I boarded the plane I was blissfully unaware of this.

The flight was pleasant and as we approached London the pilot flew in a holding pattern, waiting for permission to land. It was at that time that I began to get organized prior to landing and looked for my passport. To my utter dismay and great surprise, I could not locate it. I commented on this to my fellow-passenger in the seat next to me. This gentleman, a veterinarian from New Zealand, sympathized with my plight and told me that I would undoubtedly have to fly back to Holland. I was not ready to accept that verdict.

As I was evaluating my options, all the while asking God for discernment and assistance, I noticed the Dutch stewardess. My hopes immediately increased for I thought that surely she would know a way to help me enter Great Britain. Unhappily, she did not believe that this could be done and told me that I would have to fly back to Holland. I decided to refuse the invitation and take my chances without a passport, thinking that a situation that is impossible with man, is not necessarily impossible with God.

As I entered the airport in search of the entrance for those with foreign passports, an elderly Dutch lady approached me and told me that she had a very big problem. She did not speak English and had no idea how she could get through passport and customs control. Could I please help her? I told her I would, while silently considering my own somewhat bigger plight.

As we were waiting in the long, slowly-moving line, I prayed for wisdom. Suddenly, my eye fell on a "British Passports Only" entrance. There was no one standing in line, and a British official just waiting for work. I instantly formed my plan. I would go confidently to this gentleman, tell him the truth, and then expect to be allowed entry. A rather incredible plan, perhaps. I quickly found a new helper for the Dutch lady and walked briskly to the entrance. Any anxiety seemed to have evaporated as I faced the British official.

What happened next is almost unbelievable, but it did happen. I looked the official in the eye and said, "Look, I have lost my passport; however, I will fill out a landing card." At the same time, I reached for my pen, ready to fill out the required document. No sooner had I spoken these few words when the official on duty replied, "Don't worry sir. Have a nice day," and he waved me on through.

Walking rapidly to the baggage area, I thanked God for this unusual entry into Great Britain. Even as I sat in a taxi en route to Liverpool Railway Station, I could not help but marvel. God had once again opened a door for me. He has repeatedly done this, and I know He will do it again and again. I take comfort from the words: "Have no fear of sudden disaster or of the ruin that overtakes the wicked, for the LORD will be your confidence . . ." (Prov. 3:25–26).

Positive Thinking is Optimistic

Overcomers look to the future. They know that circumstances change, and that, with the exception of God, nothing stays the same. They do not spend a great deal of time thinking about what they have done, but concentrate on what they are doing and will be doing. Although they live in the present, they look optimistically to the future. Inventors, explorers, writers, and researchers are good examples of individuals who are optimistic. The more optimistic they are, the more they succeed. But optimism is not limited to them. Every person, regardless of educational, professional, or social status, can be optimistic.

Nearly two decades ago I believed that God wanted me to teach others how they could best help themselves with His help. This led to the teaching of Christian self-counseling courses, the training of numerous lay-counselors, and the writing of a book. Although I was working in a very small town in northern Michigan, I was optimistic that the concept of Christian self-counseling would eventually reach many individuals around the world. In fact, the Christian self-counseling concept continues to multiply, reaching people in the U.S.A., Canada, Western Africa, Europe, the Middle East, and China. Whenever we have a calling, vision, dream, or talent, we need to explore it. Certainly, we must not be swayed by those negative thinkers who will say that something cannot be done even though we are in the middle of doing it. We had better look to God. "You, O LORD, keep my lamp burning; my God turns my darkness into light" (Ps. 18: 28–29).

Some people, however, are against the very concept of positive thinking. They believe that it minimizes the terrible things that happen to so many people—things over which they may have no control. In my opinion, however, positive thinking does not have to limit this reality at all. The overwhelming majority of people I have counseled during the past 30 years, believers and nonbelievers alike, were greatly in need of a good dose of positive thinking. They did not have too much of it; they were all too often greatly lacking in it. Of course, positive thinking must not, and cannot, take the place of realistic or rational thinking. Each type of thinking plays a distinct and equally important part in the resolution of conflict and problems, and the attainment of a variety of important goals.

The Triumph of Faith

Positive thinking, as I said earlier, though closely related to faith, is not identical to it. In this chapter I have stressed the importance of positive thinking as an integral part of wholesome thinking. Every overcomer makes use of positive thinking in one way or another. Nevertheless, it is also clear that positive thinking has its limitations and cannot begin to compete with faith, nor should it attempt to do so. Certainly no amount of positive thinking can take the place of faith. Positive thinking sometimes is open to misinterpretation. At times, regrettably, we find people so involved in positive thinking that they start to equate it with unlimited personal power.

I want to state emphatically here that no amount of positive thinking and no amount of personal power can take the place of God's power—the power of the Holy Spirit. One thing is abundantly clear: we are not *justified* (made guiltless), *purified* (cleansed from guilt), *sanctified* (made holy), and most of all not *saved* (delivered from the power and the consequences of sin) by positive thinking or any kind of personal power. Such positive thinking fails to take into account the sin in our lives. I am convinced it is only by faith that these things occur. It is by grace through faith that we are saved. Faith does not originate with man, but originates with God. Faith is a gift from God!

It is Christ who is the architect of both our faith and our salvation. It is Christ who chose us first (John 15:16), and it is by His faith that He lives within us. The Christian believer cries out with the apostle Paul ". . . I live by faith in the Son of God, who loved me and gave himself for me" (Gal. 2:20).

From faith in the triune God we receive a wonderful new outlook and worldview! It is the worldview of the Revelation of John which tells us that no matter what happens, no matter what obstacles arise or beasts stand in our way, we are on the winning side. This sense of ultimate victory now colors all our thinking. And that is the background of my focus on positive thinking.

Part Three:

The Emotional Well-Being of Overcomers

6

Overcomers Control Their Anger

Generally speaking, our emotions result from a combination of perceptions and thoughts. While this holds true most of the time for most people, it is important to understand that sometimes other variables are involved as well. In this chapter we will explore some of those variables as we consider how to eliminate the dysfunctional aspects of anger.

In this country there are millions of individuals with relatively mild emotional problems. These individuals are not dysfunctional or even significantly impaired socially. By contrast there are also those who suffer from severe emotional problems. Some have very dysfunctional backgrounds and live under such distressing conditions that it is hard for them to think clearly and thus to feel good. Others have adverse genetic or biochemical components in their physical/emotional makeup.

My point in the next three chapters, however, is that millions of people, including countless Christians, may suffer needlessly. I say *needlessly* because *if* they were better informed they might be more able to manage, or prevent, acute levels of anger, anxiety, or depression.

This matter of managing our emotions takes time to learn, because our emotions do not exist in isolation but function in the whole of our physical, mental, and spiritual life. All aspects of our being are interconnected and interdependent. We cannot think well if our brain cells do not function well, and our brain cells cannot function well if they are not fed well. They depend on a well-nourished, well-functioning body, which, in turn, depends on a healthy diet and a wholesome life-style. But we may not be very motivated to live a wholesome life if our spiritual life is in disorder. *Accordingly, all parts of our life must be managed well for us to be able to manage our emotions well.*

Understanding Anger

Normal anger is a strong reactive feeling of displeasure over real or imagined wrongs, injustices, or injuries to self or others, with or without concurrent impulses to retaliate. Of all the human emotions none is more controversial or misunderstood than the emotion of anger. Listen to the cacophony of voices on the subject: "We must never be angry: all anger is sin"; "anger can be avoided—it does not have to surface"; "anger is a wonderful way to express our feelings; it gets attention fast; it gets things done; it is important to our survival"; "anger is a social regulator, it helps us to communicate better and to protect ourselves; it prevents victimization."

Some individuals describe anger as insanity, a curse, or an evil and grossly abnormal emotion. By others, anger is heralded as helping individuals to protect their identity and integrity, and to successfully deal with hostile environments. Can we make some sense out of this cacophony? Upon closer scrutiny, could anger be a realistic, rational, or even positive emotion, endorsed by Scripture? I think the answer is yes.

Developmental and Cultural Aspects of Anger

We must begin by acknowledging that anger is one of four basic, normal human emotions, the other three being fearfulness, sadness, and happiness. Anger is universal, found everywhere, also in the Christian community. Since there is a developmental side to anger, we can count on having to deal with it throughout our lives. It is found in *infants* (giving shrill notice of their discomfort), *children* (impatient of parental restrictions or sibling aggression), *adolescents* (driven by raging hormones and profound insecurities) and *adults* (reacting to a whole range of frustrations).

Then there is the cultural aspect. In some cultures the expression of anger is highly restrained or totally taboo, a major breach of accepted standards. In other cultures the expression of anger, while not unrestrained, seems much more an expected part of life than in North America. Here, on the other hand, men are often given much more freedom to express their anger—in word or deed—than women. While the emotion of anger is universal, there is much regional variety in how and when it is expressed.

Anger can also be viewed as simply a component of an underlying mental or emotional disorder. It is commonly found, for example, in people suffering from anxiety disorders, e.g. Post-traumatic Stress Disorder, or a mood disorder called Bipolar Disorder (Manic-Depressive Disorder), substance (ab)use disorders, or certain personality disorders (Brandt, 1998, 1999).

Personality Aspects of Anger

Our personalities play a major part in certain types of anger. For example, antisocial, paranoid, and narcissistic personalities often have a lot of *aggressive anger*. Those who have antisocial personalities do not care what happens to other people. That being their attitude, they are quick to attack and explode with anger. The paranoid personality views other people as secret adversaries and therefore is supersensitive. And those with narcissistic personalities assume that they are better than others, and become explosively angry when their desire for control, attention, or position is thwarted.[1]

There is still another type of anger that deserves our notice: *constrained anger.* It is a deep-seated resentment often found, for example, in negativistic personalities. Negativistic persons, whose outlook is basically a passive-aggressive one, can be obstinate, obstructive, scornful, and sullen. They have a "need" to oppose anyone in a position of authority or influence who is capable of restricting their freedom. Even very ordinary demands made by family members, employers, or friends may ignite their anger. They live with a hidden storehouse of anger inside of them which is sure to surface under pressure.

Perhaps the worst kind of anger is *rage*. This is a violent anger rooted in deep-seated feelings of hatred and bitterness often formed in response to injustices and injuries suffered in childhood and adolescence. This rage may often smolder in victims of sexual, physical, or emotional abuse. Rage of this kind is often present in people who have a so-called borderline personality. Explosions of violent anger tend to occur more readily at times when these individuals are undergoing excessive stress. This stress may result from a variety of sources, especially frustration over difficulties in achieving closeness, connection, or control.

Anger as a negative, aggressive emotion is destructive beyond words. Just think of the physical violence that occurs in 15 percent of all marriages in the U.S., or child abuse, which affects a million children per year. So, while as a normal and healthy emotion anger is to be valued, as a negative and aggressive emotion it causes untold grief. Happily, there are many things that can be done to overcome this problem.

Normal anger is an emotion that a healthy person cannot *not* have. Any healthy human being, any "thinking" human being, from time to time experiences the basic emotions of sadness, happiness, anxiousness, and anger. There is nothing inherently wrong with anger (or else how could a holy God be angry?), anymore than there is something inherently wrong with sadness, or anxiousness, or happiness. It is what we do with our emotions that make them good or bad. Whether anger arises from physical disorders, from the experience of injustice and frustration, or personality problems, we can learn to express it in appropriate ways.

Emotional Aspects of Anger

On an emotional level there are other characteristic features associated with the experience of anger. Angry people nearly always see themselves as being crossed or victimized. Someone cuts them off in traffic; someone paints a house and is never paid; a business partner flies the coop, leaving big debts behind. In each of these cases there is an experience of loss, the loss of self-esteem, the loss of face, the loss of money, the loss of a relationship, the loss of stability in one's life. In accidents caused by drunken drivers there may be the loss of a life, the loss of an arm or a leg, the loss of skills or abilities. *In every case here, anger is a natural response.* It is a signal telling us that something wrong has happened, a signal which must not be ignored.

Anger is also found among individuals who are beset by a deep sense of helplessness or worthlessness. Not surprisingly, anger often goes hand-in-hand with depression. In both cases there is the powerful temptation simply to blame circumstances for one's bitter sense of powerlessness, as though the environment creates our emotive responses. Individuals who believe this are "sitting ducks" for the uncontrolled expression of aggressive feelings.

We need to understand that anger can be a *rational* as well as an *irrational emotion.* Often the difference is described as assertive versus aggressive anger. Let's first consider what we mean by assertive anger. Assertive anger is the kind of anger that allows us to speak freely about our convictions, defend our ethics, and stand up for the well-being of others as well as of ourselves. Many a needed social movement was sparked by this kind of assertive anger. The assertive anger I have in mind is entirely compatible with the recognition of the limitations inherent in all imperfect and sinful human beings. Assertive anger, in short, can be righteous anger.

Thinking that anger always stems from a person's irrational belief system, some hold that anger is always inappropriate. Indeed, anger is very often irrational, in origin and expression, but certainly not always. Many times anger stems from the intricate biochemical makeup of an individual, or from certain illnesses. Other times it is rooted in hormonal or nutritional deficiencies. It is therefore wrong—even irrational—to say that anger is always an inappropriate negative emotion based on a person's irrational beliefs.

Spiritual Aspects of Anger

In the Old Testament alone there are over 300 instances where God Himself is angry. At what?—At sin, human brutality and destructiveness. The apostle Paul, citing Psalm 4, sums it up by saying: "In your anger do not sin" (Eph. 4:26). That admonition is filled with inner tension, but entirely true to the reality of a holy life (cf. Prov.15: 1; 23: 24; 29:11).

Paul's dual admonition recognizes the complexity of anger. While it is true that most people, most of the time, make themselves angry by way of angry self-talk based on demands rather than wishes, it is also true that anger in human life is a very complex emotion for which there is no simple explanation. *Assertive anger is realistic, rational and positive.* It seeks to prevent or solve problems and to correct wrongs. Its aim is to impart necessary information, knowledge and wisdom. At its best it is potentially a healing, growth-producing force—as any Old Testament prophet can testify.

It is time that we stop thinking of anger as a purely destructive force, something that should be suppressed at all cost. What other emotion is there that can help us express strong feelings of displeasure, when such feelings are in order? Without the expression of displeasure many a historic wrong would have never been righted. It communicates to others the things that *are* important to us. The benefits of righteous anger, carefully expressed, are obvious. Certainly it is important to be defenders of the faith, teachers, and believers who must say "no" to a whole range of things in a culture that has lost its bearings and is torn by conflict.

Some individuals, however, believe that there is nothing useful about anger, and that it cannot resolve anything at all. These individuals are doubtless sincere, but their logic, I am afraid, runs directly counter to the evidence. I am speaking of the evidence pertaining to human behavior, the construction of the brain, and the universality of this basic emotion. I also have in mind the dangers of bottling up our anger, not expressing our annoyance over injustices, of not being upset over violence, brutality, corruption, or the abuse and starvation of innocent children.

What we need to learn, and learn quickly, is that there is indeed nothing wrong with righteous anger. There is, however, a way God intends for us to have and to express this emotion. We know that our Lord Jesus on several occasions exhibited righteous anger. In John 11—to cite one example—where we learn of Lazarus's death and burial and Jesus' reaction to the whole scene surrounding him—we read (vv. 33, 38) that Jesus was "greatly disturbed in spirit." But scholars who know the original Greek are often much more definite. They say it refers to profound anger.[2] Jesus was clearly aghast and angry at the way the mourners were allowing death to dominate their outlook. Within minutes He created a totally new situation by asserting His Lordship over death. Talk about the constructive outcome of assertive anger! This example alone should forever lay to rest the strange notion that the expression of anger is always wrong.

Now let us look at the other side of the coin. We also need to know that it is wrong when anger is in the saddle and we are controlled by it. Things also go badly awry when, thinking that to show anger is mistaken, we suppress it, turn it inward and become depressed. Anger converted into hidden but nevertheless powerful resentment may in fact lead to destructive outbursts of anger or rage and acts of violence.

Consider the consequences of *aggressive* anger. Such anger always leaves destruction in its wake because it seeks to harm, hurt, dissolve, blame, and incriminate. It provokes others to respond with anger of their own and provides pathological justification for an ever-growing circle of accumulating anger.

Physical Aspects of Anger

Anger is often a component of a larger problem such as alcohol, cocaine, or nicotine addiction or withdrawal. It is also a common component, as many women know all too well, of the so-called premenstrual syndrome. This should put us on our guard against making snap judgments about anger. In many instances of intense anger we are simply dealing with people suffering from excessive stress, hormonal imbalances, and the like. While some respond to these internal stimuli with depression or anxiety, others respond with anger. Whether this is a matter of temperament or of perceptual differences we do not always know.

One thing is clear: anger is more than a simple matter of choice. It is well-known that in some people anger is more quickly triggered when physical problems are present. In my experience as a therapist I have learned that physical variables often play a significant part in angry responses. This does not alter the fact, however, that choice remains a critical element in human emotions, including the emotion of anger. Most people, it would seem, have the freedom, at least most of the time, to think either positive or negative thoughts.

Then there are the illnesses that result from the mishandling of aggressive anger. These illnesses occur most often in those who push their anger inward. People who repress or suppress their anger may develop hives, eczema, asthma, constipation, nausea, and patterns of vomiting, ulcers, heart disease, and even cancer. Needless to say, these disorders may have other causes; I am saying, however, that people who turn their anger inward and thus fail to express this very important emotive feeling—as frequently happens in Christian circles—all too often wind up with physical disorders. So the suppression of anger, which we thought was the right thing to do, often leads to greater problems for ourselves and others, to say nothing of the medical bills that ensue.

In view of what we have said so far it is really no wonder that anger is so often misunderstood. Here we have this very basic, universally shared, normal emotion which is designed to help and not to hinder us. It enables us to communicate our true inner feelings and thoughts more effectively, to help defend ourselves more efficiently, and perhaps to ensure our very survival. But what have we done with it? We have—of all things—turned this God-given emotive feeling into a weapon of destruction, one that hurts others and that backfires upon ourselves. Even suppressing it is dangerous. And in the resulting broken relationships and ruined lives we can no longer clearly see the difference between the good emotion and the evil expression of it.

Anger is in some ways different from any other basic emotion. Lets consider some of its physiological characteristics. As an internal feeling-state, anger originates in the neocortex and limbic system of the brain. As a result of our displeasure at certain occurrences, the hypothalamus is alerted and ignites the chain reaction that prompts the release of adrenaline. This adrenaline released in the bloodstream results in such manifestations as a pounding heart, a dry mouth, feelings of faintness or dizziness, cold hands, headache, stomachache or fatigue. Sometimes it results in crying spells, a person's face will turn red, the pupils of the eyes dilate—all in conjunction with other physical manifestations. Thus, prompted by a rush of adrenaline, many physical changes occur.

Overcoming Anger

In the previous section we learned that anger is a universal emotion, something all of us have to deal with. We also learned that anger remains a much-misunderstood emotion because it has basically two faces: one constructive and the other destructive. It may be healthy but it may also be a symptom of a physical, emotional, personality, or spiritual problem.

In the previous section, too, we made a distinction between assertive and aggressive anger. It is the latter which is the primary focus of this section. Any Christian aware of the enormously destructive nature of aggressive anger will look for ways to prevent it in the first place, and effectively deal with it when it does arise. What can we do that will enable us not to let the sun go down on our anger, not to avenge ourselves, and in this context to love our neighbor as ourselves? *That* is the question we wish to address here.

Since anger is a physical, emotional and/or spiritual phenomenon, we may be in need of physical restoration, emotional re-education, and/ or spiritual regeneration. The latter is not to be overlooked. It is my experience that problems with anger may readily arise even in very spiritual persons. All human beings are vulnerable in body, mind, and spirit, and may get caught up in the constantly changing demands made on them by their internal and external environment.

Physical Intervention

If it is true—and I believe it is—that in every instance of anger there is at least a physical and an emotional component, then we need to focus on the restoration of physical as well as emotional well-being. This is not to say that spiritual well-being is of no account but it *is* to say that a person's spiritual well-being, too, is wrapped up in the ability to make sound rational judgments. Spiritual discernment simply cannot be isolated from the issues of truth, reason, and faith. While there are many aspects to the phenomenon of anger, and many possible approaches to overcoming it, I for one believe it is important to look first at a person's physical condition and concentrate on physical restoration. This is not, of course, to imply that physical health is the main condition for solving the problem of inordinate anger. Ultimately what is needed is emotional reeducation and spiritual regeneration or reorientation. But that is usually not the level at which we can begin the process.

To make sure that the necessary emotional adjustments can be made in overcoming anger we must first look at the possibility of physical problems. When there is no electricity there is no light (in our culture at least), and when there is no well-functioning body there is no well-functioning mind. Emotional reeducation is not likely to occur apart from a body and a set of brains that are at least relatively functional.

Physical conditions such as underfunctioning or overfunctioning of the thyroid gland, intoxication, or withdrawal from alcohol, caffeine or cocaine, or nicotine, is often accompanied by irritability or anger. Anger responses may also be triggered by certain neurological disorders, hormonal imbalances, nutritional deficiencies, and a wide range of illnesses—for example, rheumatoid arthritis.

Vulnerability to anger may also be found in glucose disturbances. Depending on the presence of either high or low blood sugar levels, a person may be correspondingly vulnerable to the anger response. The reasons for this phenomenon are many, including the fact that *low* blood sugar is also associated with an *increased* level of adrenal hormones. These in turn exacerbate a person's excitability and irritability, rendering this person more prone to make false judgments. Obviously those who have chronic anger problems should have a thorough physical examination. Only an experienced physician can determine if there is an underlying pathology which could make a person more susceptible to anger.

To more fully appreciate the biochemical involvement in anger arousal and responses, we need to remember the logical sequence that is involved here. First of all, whenever we perceive something, this will be registered by our brain, and in particular by the thinking portion of the brain. Once the brain has received certain signals it will respond with some kind of interpretation. We will have thoughts, beliefs, and/or emotive responses to the sensory input that has entered into our field of awareness. After a primitive interpretation of facts or events, the *thalamus* sends signals to the thinking and feeling portions of the brain, as well as to the hypothalamus (see endnotes chapters 8, 9).

From this point on an increasing chemical reaction kicks in. A chemical released by the pituitary gland stimulates the release of chemicals by the thyroid, adrenal, and other glands involved in this process of perceptions, actions, and reactions. Ultimately, the anger response consists of electrochemical responses to our perceptions and thoughts. Once physical feelings and actions are involved, signals are sent back to our brain and the whole cycle repeats and reinforces itself. Unless there is some kind of mental resolution, or some kind of physical-stress-reduction, the emotional responses will only be magnified.

If a medical examination reveals that underlying physical problems need corrective action, then perhaps some medications are all that is necessary, but more likely there will also be a need for psychological intervention. In addition to medications, a physician may recommend a program of stress-reduction with emphasis on a healthy diet, regular exercise, rest, relaxation, and recreation.

Psychological Intervention

Whatever the primary source of aggressive anger, all forms of it are self-defeating. Ultimately aggressive anger is based on thinking errors and self-defeating beliefs. *In order to overcome aggressive anger we must remove errors in our thinking and replace self-defeating beliefs.* Realistic, rational, and positive evaluations, interpretations, and self-talk are needed to overcome our anger. (See chapters 3, 4, 5, 9, and 11).

If we are controlled by anger we undoubtedly feel uncomfortable with ourselves and others. To overcome this persistent sense of discomfort we must let go of the idea that we can be perfect, and accept ourselves and others as fallible human beings. To feel more comfortable with other people we must learn to hold on to our values and beliefs and be able to associate with others without necessarily endorsing their lifestyles or beliefs (cf. 1 Cor. 5:9, 10). In fact, we may reject the latter, and do so without anger or bitterness.

Those who have problems controlling their anger often feel impelled to control, overpower, and punish others. Obviously, we must let go of any tendencies in this direction. It is bad for everyone concerned. We must especially look to our own follies, fears, and failures as the primary source of our anger and unhappiness. Once we discover that it is more advantageous to have self-control and self-direction, as well as proof of the presence of God in our lives (Titus 1:8; 2:5, 6, 12; Gal. 5:23), we are perhaps more ready to examine solutions.

In order to overcome aggressive anger—or any other emotional problem—it is best to *focus* on the solution, rather than the problem. How we can get along better with others? How can we deal in a more life-enhancing manner with objective reality around us? The following are some helpful steps in the process of emotional reeducation:

Intellectual Insight. We must recall that *all* people are imperfect, fallible and sinful creatures. Even the most mature Christians have only a small beginning of what the Lord intends them to become. To overcome our aggressive anger it is absolutely no use waiting for our environment, or the people we live with or work for, to change. It is we who need to change. Why do we need to change? For one thing, because that is the red-hot thrust of the gospel of Christ (cf. Matt 4:17; Mark 1:15; Luke 13:3; Acts 2:38).

For another, because it is in our best interest to replace self-defeating beliefs with life-enhancing beliefs.

Correct Practice. We need to immediately practice new behaviors that go with our new insights. Supreme among these new behaviors is wholesome self-talk.[3] Wholesome self-talk—what does that sound like? Here are a few samples:

- "I am a fallible human being, neither superior nor inferior. I aim to do my rational best in giving my utmost to God's highest. I know this is God-glorifying and I trust it will increase my happiness. I will do this for the rest of my earthly life."
- "Facts or events do not create my feelings. I make myself happy, calm, glad, joyful, and even loving, as the result of my perceptions and thoughts.
- "I will, with God's help, make sure that my perceptions and thoughts are realistic and rational. This enables me to discover worthwhile alternatives, if need be."

Mental-Emotional Dissonance. During this third step in the process of emotional reeducation, we know that what we are doing is right, although it feels wrong. At this stage many people erroneously believe they cannot really change their beliefs or behaviors—something feels wrong or out of sync. Although we know we are doing the right thing it simply does not *feel* right.

The only way to overcome mental-emotional dissonance is to continue the correct practice anyway. It is difficult for a person who previously responded with outbursts of anger or rage to respond patiently with forgiveness and kindness, but by doing so we arrive at the next step of emotional reeducation where we experience emotional insight.

Emotional Insight. At this stage we not only *know* that the things we are saying or doing are right, but they also *feel* right. If we continue to practice them, we will eventually have the new behaviors we desire; they will become a natural response. Since most of our inappropriate anger is the result of anger-specific self-talk, it is important to thoroughly study chapter 9, *Overcomers Lead Happier Lives*, where we can learn how to have more emotional control.

The Power of the Tongue

We must remember that there is a major difference between sources and causes. *Sources*, which are around us in great abundance, can only become *causes* of anger if we let them. While betrayal or deception are obvious sources over which we can greatly upset ourselves, we still have a choice and a voice in the matter. Our thoughts, beliefs, and attitudes have everything to do with how we perceive and think about external sources. As Christians we have resources that are more than adequate to help us cope with the challenges of life: the Word of God that is very near, "in our mouth and in our heart" (cf. Deut.30:14).

The majority of our physical and emotional problems, including anger, are not only created by our own thoughts and beliefs but kept alive by constantly talking about them. We tell ourselves how we are being victimized by circumstances; we tell ourselves that life is horrible and that people are bad; we tell ourselves that things have never been worse than they are today; we tell ourselves all these depressing and angering things and then believe ourselves. But this is not how our heavenly Father would have us think.

> Plagues and deaths around me fly;
> Till he bids, I cannot die;
> Not a single shaft can hit
> Till the God of love sees *fit*.
> John Ryland (1752–1825)

Spiritual Intervention

It will be very difficult, however, to think and speak right, unless we are born again spiritually. The latter is essential before we can truly overcome all vestiges of dysfunctional anger. God is *the* antidote to aggressive, irrational, or other forms of dysfunctional anger. But even if we have been "saved by grace," we still have work to do. God wants us to be participators in His kingdom. The Word of God is our final authority whenever we wish to root out destructive behaviors of any kind. Here He reminds us that we must change our *cruelty* into *kindness*; *rudeness* into *politeness*; *ridicule* into *respect*; *persecution* into *support*; *contempt* into *courtesy*; *condemnation* into *pardon*; *hatred* into *love*, and *aggressive anger* into *peaceful self-control*.

Listen to the apostle Paul: "Therefore each of you must put off falsehood and speak truthfully to his neighbor, for we are all members of one body. 'In your anger do not sin.' Do not let the sun go down while you are still angry, and do not give the devil a foothold. . . . Do not let any unwholesome talk come out of your mouths, but only what is helpful for building others up according to their needs, that it may benefit those who listen. And do not grieve the Holy Spirit of God, with whom you were sealed for the day of redemption. Get rid of all bitterness, rage and anger, brawling and slander, along with every form of malice. Be kind and compassionate to one another, forgiving each other, just as in Christ God forgave you" (Eph. 4:25–32).[4]

7

Overcomers Manage Their Anxieties

Anxiety is an emotive feeling that is experienced by all normal people at one time or another. At times, however, anxiety can be disabling and painful. There are many physical, psychological, and spiritual sources for anxiety. All too often these sources are overlooked and many individuals suffer needlessly from preventable anxiety. Others may not recognize that they have an anxiety *disorder* for which treatment is usually available. This chapter explains the differences between normal and disabling anxiety, and describes some helpful physical, emotional, and spiritual antidotes.

Anxiety, both as a normal emotive feeling and as a disabling condition, remains largely misunderstood in our society. Any form of anxiety, regardless of its severity, is all too often seen as something abnormal—perhaps as some kind of personal weakness. Some individuals even believe that it is best to never show any sign of anxiety. And that in spite of the fact that all individuals experience some form of anxiety from time to time. Here I am speaking mainly about so-called normal anxiety—*a feeling of apprehensiveness, or uneasiness, about some unclear demand or a possible threat.*

It is also important to make a clear distinction between fear and anxiety. Fear is situation-specific. Whether real or imagined, we know *what* we are afraid of. With anxiety, however, we are not exactly sure why we feel the way we do. We may not have any clue whatsoever! We only know *that* we are afraid. Normal anxiety is a universal emotion that may at times be helpful, it may spur us into needed action, prevent us from making costly mistakes, or fulfill some other useful task. It is not disabling and does not interfere with our general happiness—at least not to any noteworthy extent.

Occasional feelings of apprehension or increased tension usually disappear without any special treatment. They simply come and go. Upon closer examination, however, we may discover that there are reasons for our normal anxiety, including some of the pressures and demands of everyday life.

Understanding Anxiety
Anxiety as Primarily a Thinking Problem

Some common thinking errors that may induce anxiety include arbitrary inferences, catastrophizing, and overgeneralization.

Arbitrary Inferences. Arbitrary inferences are assumptions which are treated as if they were facts. A person merely assumes something and then clings to that assumption without any further ado. This practice may bring much harm to ourselves, as well as to others.

Some individuals who make arbitrary inferences work hard to make their assumptions come true. Those who have negativistic, paranoid, or borderline personality styles, for example, are often quite ingenious in this regard. Because they expect the worst they may provide the incentive for someone to act in the way that they expected he or she would act, and when they succeed in doing this it provides them with reinforcement to substantiate their false assumptions.

Catastrophizing. Catastophizing is overemphasizing the worst possible outcome of something. A person, for example, notices a skipped heartbeat and believes that it is deadly. Another person has a feeling of unreality and thinks it is a sign of going crazy. A school bus is overdue and a parent is convinced that it has been in an accident. A person has the sniffles and believes it is a serious case of the flu, which will lead to pneumonia, and worse. Someone does not greet us in the street and we are convinced that person dislikes us. The worst is always going to happen!

Overgeneralization. Overgeneralization refers to the false assumption that because something has occurred once it will always reoccur. If something bad happened in one situation, it is also going to happen in other situations. Or because something felt uncomfortable, it is dangerous and to be avoided at all cost. A man makes a mistake, then claims that he never does anything right.

There is no doubt that faulty thinking is the main culprit behind much of our unwanted anxiety. To more fully appreciate how thinking errors may lead to self-defeating behaviors and painful emotional experiences, it is useful to review the *common thinking disorders* listed in Chapter 9. Faulty thinking, however, is by no means the only source of normal or disabling anxiety. Many a person suffers from anxiety caused by some readily overlooked factor. Some individuals, for example, are so sensitive to *any* amount of caffeine that even one cup of coffee, or any other product with caffeine in it, may result in feelings of tension and apprehension, or worse. Let's take a look at this.

Anxiety as Primarily a Physical Problem

At times faulty thinking is superimposed on existing physical problems, and at other times we unwittingly add physical problems to our faulty thinking. Anxiety may originate in any one of about 50 different physical sources. These sources of anxiety can broadly be divided into *neurological problems,* e.g., migraines or multiple sclerosis; *systemic disorders*, e.g. cardiovascular disease or anemia; *endocrine disturbances,* e.g., thyroid or adrenal dysfunctions; *inflammatory disease,* e.g., lupus or rheumatoid arthritis; *toxic conditions*, e.g., amphetamine or caffeine sensitivities; *allergic reactions*, e.g., environmental pollutants or food sensitivities; *nutritional factors*, e.g., vitamin or mineral deficiencies, and scores of other physical sources. (Brandt, 1999).

Even a rudimentary review of the physical sources of anxiety reminds us that it is folly to think that anxiety is *always* self-induced. In my professional experience over the past 30 years I have noticed, for example, that many anxiety sufferers also have problems with low or irregular blood sugar levels. At times I have found that low blood sugar was the primary physical source of the anxiety, and at other times that it was a *coexisting* condition, perhaps even the result of a person's anxiety. Over the years I have noticed that nearly all anxiety sufferers have one or more physical problems coexisting with faulty thinking and/or spiritual problems, but whether or not anxiety's primary source is physical, mental, or spiritual, matters little—all three areas need to be addressed.

One common problem among those who suffer from mild, moderate, or even severe anxiety, is a condition known as *Mitral Valve Prolapse* (MVP).[1] About fifty percent of all anxiety sufferers are believed to have this condition; often in conjunction with other physical problems. At the same time, it is not true that everyone who has MVP develops an anxiety problem. There are far more individuals in this country who have MVP, than those who have anxiety *disorders*. Roughly only about one in four persons who have MVP suffers from anxiety disorders. And even then it may not be the primary source of a person's anxiety. Even if it is the primary *source,* it may not be the primary *cause.* The *cause* nearly always is the result of misinterpreting the physical symptoms of MVP as something catastrophic.

Differentiating Between Sources and Causes of Anxiety

The *source* of anxiety may be physical, but the *cause* may be emotional, due to the misinterpretation of, for example, unpleasant (but harmless) sensations of fluttering feelings in the chest, palpitations, or dizziness. Some individuals with MVP are also very sensitive to caffeine, or medications with ephedrine or pseudoephedrine. There are, however, many things that can be done to deal successfully with Mitral Valve Prolapse, or any of a number of bothersome but benign physical conditions. Sound medical advice is what is needed here.

Anxiety, whether of the normal or disabling variety, like all emotive feelings, is a multifaceted phenomenon. For one thing, it is often related to excessive stress. And let me hasten to add that many things are stressful—for example, sin is stressful. And so is the use of nicotine, living in a high density neighborhood or near a metropolitan airport, being exposed to chemical pollutants or other toxins, being in bondage to an unhealthy personality—our own *or* someone else's, and hundreds of other possible stressors.

One thing is fairly clear: we do not automatically become anxious because of some *external* source, but more likely because of an *internal* focus. It is important that we consider both *sources* and *causes* of anxiety. In the final analysis, however, more often than not, we become anxious because of the way in which we react with our body, mind, and/or spirit to potential stressors. It is our inability or unwillingness to successfully deal with potential stressors that result in a loss of physical balance, psychological integrity, and/or spiritual direction. As I said earlier, not all persons with Mitral Valve Prolapse develop an anxiety disorder, and neither do all individuals who have problems with low blood sugar, poverty, allergies, nagging spouses, or any other possible source of anxiety. It is known, for example, that an infusion of lactate may cause panic attacks, but only in susceptible individuals. Anxiety is indeed a multifaceted phenomenon. And it is also an extensive and expensive problem.

It is an extensive problem because about ten percent of the U.S. population suffers from disabling anxiety *disorders*. It is considered a major health problem in this country. Not only do we have millions of sufferers consuming as many as five billion doses of tranquilizers every year (costing billions of dollars) in hopes of finding some relief, but the overall problem is on the increase. It seems that unless we return to the common sense standards set by God, learn to have more respect for our bodies as the "temple of the Holy Spirit" (1 Cor. 3:16–17), and live both more holy *and* wholesome lives, it is folly to expect that prescription drugs by themselves can solve the problem. It won't happen!

Anxiety Disorders: Disabling and Painful

In order to better understand anxiety *disorders,* I will briefly describe panic, generalized anxiety, phobic, obsessive-compulsive, and posttraumatic stress disorder—all of which require professional help.

Panic Disorder. Panic Disorder, which is twice as common in women as in men, consists of recurrent panic attacks, and worry about new attacks. Panic attacks are rather frightening, unsuspected, and unpredictable episodes of an all-encompassing, overwhelming fear. A panic attack can be mild and may only consist of severe apprehension, but more commonly it is a feeling of sheer terror, impending doom, and even death. Panic Disorder may also go hand-in-hand with agoraphobia, which is an irrational fear of public places, where it is thought that help may not be readily available. Agoraphobia, which may exist separately from panic disorder, keeps many sufferers needlessly housebound.

Generalized Anxiety Disorder. Generalized Anxiety Disorder manifests itself as an unrealistic, pervasive apprehensiveness and worry about two or more activities or events during a six-month period or longer. The tension and apprehensiveness is often accompanied by trembling, twitching, feeling shaky, muscle tension, aches and soreness, restlessness, and tiredness. Other symptoms include dizziness, light-headedness, dry mouth, flushes or chills, shortness of breath, palpitations, and nausea. Persons with Generalized Anxiety Disorder are keyed-up. They are tense, on edge, and have problems with sleeping and irritability. They are vigilant, hyperactive, apprehensive, and may also have problems with wrong thinking and self-defeating beliefs. It is the most common anxiety disorder. Again, in many cases it is due to excessive stress.

Phobic Disorder. Phobic Disorder is diagnosed in those individuals who have intense, unrealistic, and disabling fears of certain objects or situations. Consequently they have a powerful need to avoid them. In *Specific Phobia* there is a disabling fear of specific things such as elevators, heights, animals, and so forth. Whenever the person is face-to-face with the feared object there is an anxiety response. Specific phobias are universally found, may have a biological predisposing (preparedness) basis, and are subtly reinforced every time a person withdraws from the feared situation. It is considered a disorder only if there is true and lasting distress.

In *Social Phobia* (Social Anxiety Disorder), individuals suffer from unrealistic and irrational fears of being observed and evaluated by others. They think that they will not measure up to this scrutiny and are afraid of embarrassment and humiliation. Thus they prefer to blend into the background and be as inconspicuous as possible.

It has been suggested that some phobias may have a physical source on which individuals superimpose fearful perceptions and interpretations. Physical sources possibly include inner ear malfunction, allergies, and/or blood sugar irregularities.

Obsessive-Compulsive Disorder. Obsessive-Compulsive Disorder is only diagnosed if the condition brings a great deal of distress, is time consuming, and interferes seriously with our daily routines, such as our job, social activities, and interpersonal relations. *Obsessions* are intrusive (unwanted) and recurring thoughts which seem irrational, yet they also seem uncontrollable. *Compulsions* are irresistible impulses to repeat some ritualistic act, for example repeatedly counting, checking, or aligning things. The performance of the ritualistic act reduces the anxiety level, where failure to do so increases it. Persistent worry is an obsession. Uncontrollable and repetitive urges are compulsions. The obsession or compulsion must be disabling or consume at least one hour each day before being diagnosed an Obsessive-Compulsive Disorder.

Posttraumatic Stress Disorder. Posttraumatic Stress Disorder is a fairly disabling anxiety disorder, which occurs in the aftermath of a truly traumatic event. The *delayed reliving of a previous trauma* can be a war experience, natural disaster, major accident, serious victimization (such as rape or incest), or other trauma. The events may be relived consciously or in dreams. A diagnosis of Posttraumatic Stress Disorder is only made if the traumatic event is persistently reexperienced and the stimuli associated with the event are avoided. Thoughts associated with this disorder may include those of a "foreshortened" future, for example, the person may not expect to have a career, marriage, or long life. Symptoms include irritability, outbursts of anger, sleep and concentration problems, startle responses, and hypervigilance. These disturbing symptoms must have been present for at least a month before a diagnosis can be made. Posttraumatic Stress Disorder is experienced by less than one percent of the population and is twice as common in women as in men.

Anxiety as Primarily a Spiritual Problem

Few people would dispute that both mind and body play a major role in the creation and resolution of anxiety. It is, however, folly to overlook our relationship to God. Regrettably, there are all too many Christians who fail to heed the warning that they are to live without care: "Do not fret *or* have any anxiety about anything, but in every circumstance *and* in everything, by prayer and petition (definite requests), with thanksgiving, continue to make your wants known to God" (AMP Phil. 4:6).

In my work, and elsewhere, I meet many Christians who lead defeated lives. Some of them are anxious persons who worry excessively about material things, possessions, power, status, influence, or control. Or, I meet those who have fearful, weary, unstable, withdrawn, helpless, or resistant *personality styles*. The painful anxiety that these individuals needlessly endure would dissipate if they wholeheartedly placed their trust in God: "You will keep in perfect peace him whose mind is steadfast, because he trusts in you" (Isa. 26:3).

Many secular persons suffer from deep anxiety as soon as they lose their "faith" in the materialistic and temporal world—a world which is bound to disappoint them sooner or later. In their despair they cry out, "Where is the meaning of life?" "What is the purpose of living?" "Who will fill this void within me?" "Where is justice and fairness?" And they draw the conclusion that the world is an uncertain, fearful, lonely, and dangerous place. In the meantime, wrong thinking has kept them away from the eternal truth of the Gospel.

Blinded by doubt, envy, fear, greed, hostility, and jealousy they have failed to see the light of liberation. They have missed the call and tug on their heart that they must love others selflessly, lay down their life in order to find it, and give rather than receive.

These individuals will feel uneasy and remain apprehensive until such time that they no longer have to fear anything in this life or the life to come. And that, of course, can only happen when they realize that they are lost and need to be found by Him who called on them in the first place. For it is Christ Himself who wants to liberate every anxious person (Matt. 6:25–34).

While unbelievers may suffer unnecessary anxiety because of a *God-void,* we find some Christians who are suffering from anxiety because of *God-neglect,* or *God-confusion.* While nonbelievers worry about nothingness, Christians may feel apprehensive because they have been disobedient to the will of God. They have *neglected* to think right, that is, with the reasoning power of love, and the loving power of reason. They have moved away from the source of love and are trapped by fear: "There is no fear in love. But perfect love drives out fear, because fear has to do with punishment. The one who fears is not made perfect in love" (1 John 4:18).

But to be human is to be deeply troubled at times. Anxiety is part of the human condition. The writer of the book of Job is also sure of this: ". . . man is born to trouble as surely as the sparks fly upward" (Job 5:7). The apostle Paul confessed: "We are hard pressed on every side . . ." (2 Cor. 4:8). And Peter assured his readers, ". . . for a little while you may have had to suffer grief . . . in all kinds of trials." (1 Pet. 1:6). Thus there has to be once again a dividing line, between what is normal and what is disabling anxiety. For Christians it is not normal to think that God has left or forsaken them, for the exact opposite holds true: "Never will I leave you; never will I forsake you" (Heb. 13:5). For Christians it is necessary to take full responsibility for their feelings. Elsewhere I have described it this way:

> . . . the Scriptures (also) show that, as long as believers look hourly to God for help, they can overcome troubles, trials, temptations, and whatever other difficulties they encounter. Thus the threat does not come from the side of God. Nor does the threat arise from the fact of our losses. Loss—of our possessions, friends, health, loved ones, or whatever—by itself cannot bring us to despair. *It is what we tell ourselves in the situation of loss that makes the difference* (Brandt, 1988).

Our spiritual nature is closely intertwined with our psychological nature, and the latter is dependent on a well-functioning body. It can readily be seen that at times spiritual confusion may be affected by our mental/emotional condition. Although separate entities, there are no dividing walls between spirit, mind, and body. In order to deal with any kind of anxiety it is necessary to pay proper attention to all three. It is wise to remember the totality of our personhood. The apostle Paul reminds us that our ". . . whole spirit, soul and body be kept blameless . . ." (1 Thess. 5:23).

Overcoming Anxiety

The main purpose for this section is to compliment the help that is available from competent professionals. It provides a limited overview of a few practical steps in overcoming anxiety problems—some physical, emotional, and spiritual antidotes to anxiety.

Let me emphasize that anyone who has *disabling* anxiety needs to seek professional help without delay, and if necessary obtain a second, or even a third, opinion. Anxiety is an eminently treatable condition, but too many anxiety sufferers fail to obtain the help that is available.

Physical Antidotes

Medication. Anyone who suffers with anxiety problems must ensure that all possible physical sources for this are identified and treated without delay. If the anxiety is thought to be disabling, the physician has a choice of several effective medications. Most anti-anxiety drugs are prescribed by non-psychiatrists. The overwhelming majority of persons with anxiety are treated by a variety of medical professionals. The average physician certainly has plenty of experience in dealing with anxious patients.

The choice of the medication depends on the type of anxiety disorder that is being diagnosed. For Panic Disorder and Agoraphobia, Social Phobia, Generalized Anxiety, Posttraumatic Stress Disorder, and Obsessive-Compulsive Disorder, different medications are available. Physicians also often prefer some form of psychotherapy in conjunction with pharmacotherapy. This may include behavior, cognitive, family, or supportive therapy. Some anxiety disorders, for example, Posttraumatic Stress Disorder and phobias, are often treated primarily with psychotherapy. Much of this depends on a physician's point of view. While medical treatment may bring some quick relief, by itself it is *not* the final answer to the anxiety problem.

Stress Reduction. The medical model, however, is not the only available physical approach in dealing with anxiety. A nonmedical approach to reduce physical vulnerability believes that excessive stress is the primary source of the problem. The beauty of this model is that it consists of sound health practices that are useful for all individuals. I have found that stress reduction is indeed a formidable weapon against anxiety of any kind. Very often, *physical stress* is the primary source for anxiety problems. But, even if the primary source is mental or spiritual, we still *must* reduce physical stress *and* improve our overall physical health. Even in His dealings with Jonah (Jonah 4:6) and other biblical characters, God often ministered first to their bodies (John 21:12; Matt. 15:32).

Sound Nutrition is Essential

Earlier I said that at times anxiety is superimposed on existing physical problems, such as multiple sclerosis, anemia, adrenal dysfunction, lupus, caffeine sensitivity, and so forth. Happily, in most cases of anxiety we find that there are no underlying serious health concerns. What we do more readily find, however, is that in many instances anxiety is directly related to improper nutrition. This does not mean that we become anxious without forming anxious thoughts or images in our brain—we don't. But it does mean that it is far easier to make ourselves upset—over just about anything—if our brain cells are starving for food. Every one of the billions of brain cells depends on sound nutrition for proper functioning.

I have been convinced for many years that, with proper nutrition and other healthy life-style measures, it is a lot easier to overcome anxiety problems. Sadly, very few mental health professionals bother to look into the relationship of food and mood. In the meantime, however, we find that the consumption of alcohol, caffeine, nicotine, and sugar often prepares the way for anxiety problems

(Brandt, 1999). Unsatisfactory dietary habits such as skipping breakfast, eating junk food (for example—cookies, candy, and donuts), consuming caffeine, and so forth—especially combined with work addiction and stressful lifestyles—are a common source (not cause) of anxiety problems. At the end of Chapter 9 are some guidelines for healthy nutrition that, in my opinion, are important for a well-functioning brain and mind.

Proper Breathing is Important

Anxious people usually don't breathe very well.[2] They are regularly shortchanged of essential oxygen for body and brain. Improper breathing is damaging to our overall health and directly affects good posture, voice control, physical complexion, and all vital bodily functions. Proper breathing, on the other hand, helps with the regulation of blood pressure, cardiac functioning, and endorphin levels. Improper posture itself, of course, may lead to poor breathing, and poor breathing in turn may increase poor posture.

The main objective of breathing is to get bad air (carbon dioxide) out of our lungs, and good air (oxygen) into our lungs. Oxygen is essential to keep our trillions of body cells alive, produce cell energy, and build new cells. Without oxygen the brain stops functioning and life ceases. Because of shallow breathing, body and brain may be oxygen-deprived. This may contribute to such physical problems as shortness of breath, reduced muscle strength, a weakened immune system, and to mental/emotional problems such as fuzzy thinking, irritability, moodiness, nervousness, and fearfulness.

Poor breathing is usually a learned bad habit. Babies breathe perfectly fine—with their whole torso—in slow and easy movements, deeply and evenly. They still use their breathing muscle—the diaphragm—wisely. Incidentally, the breathing muscle is located between our chest and abdominal wall cavity. Good breathing consists of *slowly* inhaling and exhaling through the nostrils. With good breathing we are able to feel and see the abdomen expand without strain of any kind. To learn how to do this, we can place one hand on the abdomen and the other on the chest to monitor our progress.

After we have learned to breathe properly on a fairly regular basis, then we are more ready to learn that we can *calm down by slowing our breathing down*. This can be done in many different ways, but I will mention just one method. In order to calm down, deeply inhale through the nose to the count of three (1,2,3), then slowly exhale to the count of six (1,2,3,4,5,6). Even a few minutes of a simple breathing exercise such as this will prove to be helpful. By slowing down our breathing we are literally calming ourselves down. Then after we have calmed down, we are more able to take additional anxiety-reducing steps. This might include some of the emotional antidotes I will now describe.

Emotional Antidotes

All of us have had some kind of emotional education. Regrettably, much of this is not working for us. What we may need is emotional *reeducation*. Most of our emotional and physical difficulties are the outcome of wrong thinking and wrong living. We create our emotions by the way in which we perceive, think, and speak. Our Lord, too, has taught—at least by implication—that we make ourselves anxious, and He commands us to stop this (Matt. 6:25, 31, 34). I will return to the spiritual aspects in a moment.

Remove Cognitive Distortions. Cognitive distortions—errors in our thinking—are a very common source of anxiety problems. Those who suffer from anxiety, for example, frequently use arbitrary inferences, catastrophizing, dichotomous thinking, emotional reasoning, magnification, and personalization. We need to challenge and replace these anxiety-creating thoughts in our minds with more appropriate thinking. To identify and challenge cognitive distortions we can use self-talk verification.

Self-Talk Verification. This consists of asking three simple questions: Is what I am saying *realistic*? Is what I am saying *rational*? Is what I am saying *positive*? Self-talk verification and replacement, if applicable, with wholesome alternative self-talk is a powerful reeducative step. In this process, we can also write out or record a wholesome self-talk script, which, in turn, can be committed to memory through mental practice, and then prayerfully used in actual practice. For more details on how to do this, and for examples of *thinking errors,* see Chapter 9.

Spiritual Antidotes

There are many important antidotes against anxiety, such as medications, a wellness diet, a sensible life-style, correct breathing and so forth. But none of these measures is, of course, as powerful an antidote against self-induced anxiety as God Himself! The Scriptures remind us that God is *the* antidote to anxiety.

In bad times as, as well as in good times, we are reminded to "first seek the kingdom of heaven" (Matt. 6:33). The apostle Paul tells us that whenever we are anxious we are to go to our heavenly Father in prayer, and to do so with thanksgiving (Phil. 4:6).

Who would not want to go to a loving father? More than once in my childhood I have had my anxieties assuaged by my earthly father. How well do I remember the time when I was seriously ill and my father told me that he had placed my name on God's altar and that I could stop being anxious about my health. As I trusted in my earthly father I was also shown trust in my heavenly Father, except more so. For with God nothing is impossible.

Human beings, all human beings, are troubled on every side. And this holds especially true for those who have a *God-void* and walk without guidance on this dangerous planet. Christians too are "troubled on every side, but are not distressed," as we read in the Scriptures (2 Cor. 4:8). They are not left without guidance, comfort, or hope! They really can face and deal with agonizing emotions. This is what Maarse writes:[3]

> Whatever a person fears deeply brings him into bondage; brings him into slavery. Whether this is a fear of poverty, people, a mocking world, shame, pain, illness, old age, or death—any one of these things can make him a slave of fear. But, for all of these fears the Gospel has provided liberation. Someone who is in true communion with God cannot, even at a moment of dreadful apprehension, be a slave of either passion or emotion. I don't say, he *will* not, but in accordance with the Holy Scriptures, I say he *cannot.* One who (*sub specie aeternitatis*) is

sure of his Christian faith, of what he is, who he is, whose he is, and what his destination is, who truly has been redeemed, saved by Truth, as taught by Jesus, who Himself is the Truth, *cannot* defile himself, *cannot* be mean, *cannot* lower himself, or be dragged along by passions. He *cannot* be subdued by fear, but can manage it, or even overcome it.

Maarse's position may at first glance seem rather strong, but as we look at God's Word, we quickly discern that he is entirely correct. In the Sermon on the Mount, Jesus teaches very clearly that we are not to make ourselves anxious about anything concerning our life, but rather to first seek God's kingdom (Matt. 6:33).

But, as always, we need to look at the Word of God in its full context. Not all situations are the same. Not all human beings are the same. In fact, none are. No two individuals have the same perceptual-cognitive field, and hence no two individuals can possibly experience *anything* in an identical manner.[4]

Even Jesus, as a man, on more than one occasion showed how He experienced deep emotions. When He was angry in the temple, when He cried over Jerusalem, and when He suffered deep agony in the Garden of Gethsemane. ". . . My soul is overwhelmed with sorrow to the point of death. Stay here and keep watch with me" (Matt. 26:38). It was not so much His impending death that caused Him such deep grief, but the incredible, indescribable burden of sin that He was about to carry. The sins of the world. Our sins. My sins. No other person will ever have to undergo the anguish of Jesus. But, please note that Jesus managed and subdued his feelings.

Ultimately, we find time and time again that the anxiety-response does not depend so much on the anxiety-source as it does on its interpretation. We also know, however, that some situations are very hard to deal with. Certainly not all anxiety is sinful or inappropriate. As I said earlier, managing our emotions is not simple. But it is possible if we are ready to have that personal relationship with God that Maarse was referring to when he said, "someone who is in true communion with God cannot be a slave of either passion or emotion."

Listen to God. Communion with God is more than talking to God. It includes listening to God and obeying His will. Seeking the kingdom of heaven does not only consist of being admitted to it, but becoming a worker in that kingdom. There are no spectators in God's kingdom. We seek to find and use. And we must use the things of God in helping, serving and blessing others. When we seek and find the kingdom of heaven, and it bears fruit in our hearts, we look at life from a fresh perspective—one that is perhaps similar to that of Helen Keller, Corrie Ten Boom, or Joni Eareckson-Tada, one that reflects a Christ-centered winning attitude, based on truth, reason, faith, and love.

To have suffered the frightening emptiness of total darkness and utter silence, the agony of torture and imprisonment, the desperateness of complete physical immobility and dependent helplessness, and then not only to manage our anxieties but to conquer them, is not something human beings can do by themselves. It can be done only one way: by listening closely to our Lord when He gently speaks to our hearts and says, ". . . do not worry about your life . . ."(Matt. 6:25), and as we do exactly as the apostle Paul exhorts us to do, namely, not to worry about anything at all (Phil. 4:6).

Anxious? Worried? Fearful? Apprehensive? Then first seek the kingdom of God, but remember, as Haddon W. Robinson (1991) so aptly points out:

> To seek His kingdom is to seek His work in the world. To seek His righteousness is to live the kind of life that pleases Him, which leads to another truth about righteousness. It has to do with our relationship to others. A righteous life seeks the highest good for others. Whether we deal with foes or friends, we seek their highest good because that is what God does. In business affairs or family affairs we are to seek the best for others. As we seek what is best for others, God gives us what is best for ourselves. And so we must choose. Will we continue to worry about our own needs or will we decide instead to fasten on God and His kingdom and trust Him to give us what we need?

How can we succeed when surrounded by darkness, when imprisoned, when immobilized? By crying out to God. By submitting ourselves to His will. By fervent prayer. For God Himself, in the person of the Holy Spirit, will minister to us. He truly is the antidote to our anxiety.

The Holy Spirit: Comforter, Helper, and Healer
No one can be an overcomer in Christ without the help of the Holy Spirit. He is the common denominator in the lives of all Christian overcomers who have conquered overwhelming problems. What we cannot do in our own power, can be done by the power of the Holy Spirit. It is the Holy Spirit who gave courage to Stephen, even as he was being stoned. It is the Holy Spirit who stood by Helen Keller, Corrie Ten Boom, and Joni Eareckson-Tada. It is the Holy Spirit who enables us to manage and subdue our anxieties. We can only stop worrying about ourselves, and not be afraid of anything, by the power of the Holy Spirit.

We must not forget that every believer has the Holy Spirit. But, the Holy Spirit does not work by Himself. Everything He does is done on behalf of our Savior, who in turn does nothing apart from the power of our heavenly Father. We cannot have the "true communion" with the Father and the Son, of which Maarse spoke earlier, except by the Holy Spirit. It is the Holy Spirit who pleads with us to let go of our troubles and let God take care of our anxieties. He is the One who challenges us to seek the kingdom of heaven. And it is to be a kingdom of love, peace, and joy!

The Holy Spirit helps us to find the kingdom of heaven and to be in constant prayer. Not just once a day at some preestablished time, but constant prayer. Praying upon every possible occasion—about things large or small—and to do so with a worshipful attitude and gratitude to God. We are reminded to join thanksgiving with our prayers: "Do not be anxious about anything, but in everything by prayer and petition, with thanksgiving, present your requests to God" (Phil. 4:6).

God does not need to hear from us so that He may know what we need. Of course, He already knows! He knows this better than we know it ourselves. But our heavenly Father wants to hear from us directly. He wants to have fellowship with us. He wants us to express our affection toward Him and our dependence upon Him. In so doing we become the immediate and long-term beneficiaries of His grace and mercy. We will receive the peace of God—a greater good than anything else that we could desire: "And the peace of God, which transcends all understanding, will guard your hearts and your minds in Christ Jesus" (Phil. 4:7). This peace will keep us from going down under a heavy load of fears, worries, or anxieties. It is a peace that can transform our turbulent hearts into tranquil ones: "You will keep in perfect peace him whose mind is steadfast because he trusts you" (Isa. 26:3).[5]

8

OVERCOMERS DEFEAT THEIR DEPRESSIONS

Millions of individuals are suffering from acute or chronic depression. This chapter shows that depression is a multifaceted body-mind-spirit disorder, which may be remedied with physical restoration, emotional reeducation, and/or spiritual regeneration.

Depression is an epidemic that plagues millions of individuals, many of whom have tried in vain to overcome this condition. Still, with the help of God, and a solution-focused approach, depression is a conquerable problem. To do so, however, we must pay close attention to the physical, psychological, and spiritual aspects of depression.

Understanding Depression
Physical Sources of Depression
Physical sources of depression are only *potential* stressors. These sources include allergies, amino-acid deficiencies, disease, drugs, heredity, hormonal disturbances, malnutrition, mineral deficiencies, neurotransmitter deficiencies or malfunctions, overstimulation, poisoning, trauma, understimulation, and vitamin deficiencies.

Potential stressors may eventually create a loss of physical balance. The latter is often the result of an excessive number of alarm calls to and from the hypothalamus (see illustration on page 97). The hypothalamus, which is closely connected to the limbic (feeling) system of the brain, may be seen as a kind of "switchboard" between our mind and body, and vice versa. Too many emergency calls from this switchboard tends to create problems for our adrenal (stress) glands and predispose us to depression as explained below:

Overfunctioning of the Adrenal Cortex. An excessive number of alarm calls to the hypothalamus may result in an over-functioning of the outer portion of the adrenal glands—the adrenal cortex. This may lead, among other things, to excessively high levels of cortisol, and consequently to reduced levels of the amino acid tryptophan, which is followed by reduced levels of a brain chemical known as serotonin. The latter is an important energy source for attaining or sustaining a happy frame of reference. Low levels of serotonin are implicated in some types of depression. I will return to this subject later.

Underfunctioning of the Adrenal Cortex. The continued bombardment of the adrenal cortex with "alarm calls" eventually results in an underfunctioning of the adrenal cortex. This, in turn, may lead to low levels of cortisol. When this takes place there may be an excessive utilization of glucose, which creates low blood sugar levels. When our blood sugar levels drop too low, or become too erratic, then emotional difficulties such as depression are more likely to develop.

Overfunctioning or Underfuctioning of the Adrenal Medulla. An excessive number of alarm calls may also reach the inner portion of the adrenal glands—the adrenal medulla. This may create an overproduction of epinephrine and contribute to mania (agitation, hyperactivity, hyperexcitability, and accelerated thinking and speaking), or hypomania (a less intense form of mania). Eventually, however, the adrenal medulla underfunctions and may not produce enough epinephrine, setting the stage for depression.

Other Physical Stressors. In addition to adrenal malfunctions there are many other physical stressors that may lead to a loss of physical balance and predispose someone to depression. I believe that about 25% of depressed individuals have an underlying physical disorder as the primary source for their emotional difficulties.

One fairly common physical source is found in thyroid dysfunction. Underfunctioning of the thyroid gland (hypothyroidism) lowers cellular metabolism and interrupts adequate brain functioning. This may result in weight gain, confusion, memory problems, *and* depression. This is just one more reminder that emotional difficulties are not necessarily all spiritual, and that happiness is not always merely a matter of choice—at least not a simple one! Emotional difficulties often have a physical basis (Brandt, 1988, 1999).

Some Physical Aspects of Depression

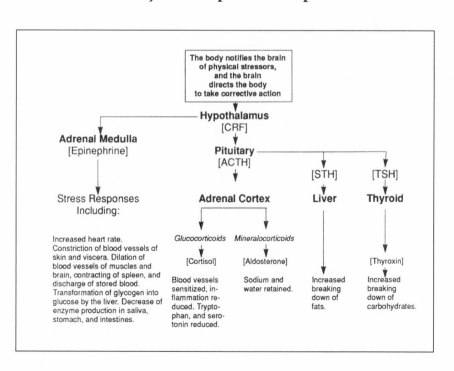

Psychological Sources of Depression

Psychological sources of depression include real or imagined *losses*. These include the loss of acceptance, confidence, employment, health, independence, love, respect, self-sufficiency, security, or trust, to name a few. We very often turn these potential stressors into actual stressors and thus create specific negative emotions, including depression. A potential psychological stressor—for example, loss of employment—may eventually lead to the disintegration of a realistic, rational, and positive belief system, and the formation of an unrealistic, irrational, and/or negative one.

A potential psychological stressor by itself, however, does not result in depression. Our perception and interpretation of facts and events—real or imagined—ultimately determine our emotive responses. If we become overwhelmed by unrealistic, irrational, or negative cognitions we lose our psychological balance. Even so, it still requires specific thoughts for specific emotions. The following illustration depicts how specific thinking leads to specific feelings.

Specific Thinking that Leads to Psychological Depression

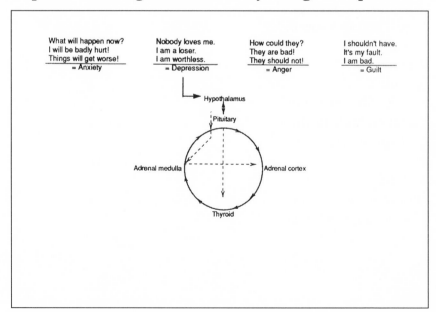

Spiritual Sources of Depression

Spiritual sources of depression include real or imagined losses, such as loss of belief in a meaningful existence, faith, hope, love, joy, peace, and so forth. A potential spiritual stressor becomes an actual stressor only when we apply unrealistic, irrational, or negative interpretations and evaluations to this loss. Spiritual depression, although potentially more destructive, is much like psychological depression. Ultimately it involves wrong thinking: the kind of thinking that is based upon the premise that the self is the center of the universe. Such self-centered thinking is a source of endless frustration, isolation, and misery. The end of that road in many cases is depression.

Spiritual depression, like physical or psychological depression, is experienced in the total person: spirit, mind, and body. Once the thinking portion of the brain registers depressive thoughts, the feeling portion of the brain is also alerted. As I said earlier, this may result in excessive alarm calls to our endocrine glands and in particular to the adrenal glands. Whatever the primary nature of the depression we find that ultimately the total person is affected.

When our spiritual perceptions and thoughts become too self-defeating, we may lose our spiritual direction. Once again, however, it requires specific thoughts to experience specific emotions. One person, for example, may willfully neglect God and become depressed, while another may do the same thing and feel anxious or guilty.

The illustration on the next page shows how the *loss* of one's mistaken faith in the things of the world; the *loss* of a sense of God's presence; or, the *loss* of the peace of God, may result in God-void, God-neglect, or God-confusion depression. Happily, spiritual depression may also signal a new beginning if the sufferer is willing to listen, either for the first time, or once again, to the gospel—a gospel of grace and mercy.

Specific Thinking that Leads to Spiritual Depression

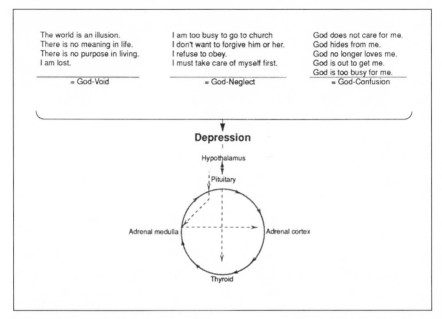

The world is an illusion.　　　I am too busy to go to church　　　God does not care for me.
There is no meaning in life.　　I don't want to forgive him or her.　God hides from me.
There is no purpose in living.　I refuse to obey.　　　　　　　　God no longer loves me.
I am lost.　　　　　　　　　　I must take care of myself first.　　God is out to get me.
　　　　　　　　　　　　　　　　　　　　　　　　　　　　　　　God is too busy for me.

= God-Void　　　　　　　　　= God-Neglect　　　　　　　　= God-Confusion

Depression

Hypothalamus

Pituitary

Adrenal medulla　　　　　　　　　　　　　　Adrenal cortex

Thyroid

The Root Sources of Depression

While there are literally hundreds of sources of depression, there are only three *root* sources. A root source is the foundation from which other things spring forth. The root sources of *depression* are *self-destructive lifestyles, self-defeating thinking,* and *self-alienation from God.* Any one of these root sources may play a role in depression. In *depressive illness,* however, we may find that possibly genetic and/or biochemical factors are the root source. Even here, however, we must be alert to such additional variables as life-style, self-defeating thinking, and sin. Remember, there is no depression, or depressive illness, that is only physical, psychological, or spiritual. Regardless of its primary nature, sooner or later depression or depressive illness affects the total person—body, mind, and spirit.

The Physical Root Source. A self-destructive life-style may include poor eating habits, self-poisoning with alcohol or nicotine, and lack of exercise, rest, or recreation. If our body is not functioning well it is difficult—and sometimes impossible—for our brain and mind to function well. Since every one of our billions of brain cells needs a steady supply of oxygen, glucose, amino acids, fatty acids, and vitamins, it is obvious that we need a sound diet and a healthy life-style.

The Psychological Root Source. Self-defeating thinking includes self-pity, other-pity, and self-blame. The majority of depressions—about 75%—are primarily the result of errors in our thinking and self-defeating beliefs. To better understand this root source see chapter 9, Overcomers Lead Happier Lives.

The Spiritual Root Source. The spiritual root source of depression is found in sin—self-alienation from God. Those who pursue a materialistic or hedonistic life-style, for example, will find themselves, sooner or later, in deep trouble. They may come to experience a devastating emptiness, which has been described as a God-void. It is the final outcome of an illusion that lasting happiness can be found in hedonism, humanism, or materialism. It is also possible to experience the love of God and then through neglect to lose the awareness of that love. This God-neglect may lead to a loss of a sense of fellowship. Sometimes we also find Christians who, for one reason or another, occasionally suffer with God-confusion. They may think and say such things as "God does not care for me," "God hides from me, "God no longer loves me," "God is too busy for me," and so forth. (cf. Ps. 13:1–3).

The Chemistry of Emotions

There are many complex electro-biochemical processes in the brain by which signals are sent from the cerebral cortex to the limbic system, and from there, mainly via the endocrine system, to the entire body. Stress warning signals from the body are also transmitted to the brain and provide an already stressed brain and mind with more to worry about. In the limbic system we find such major players as the amygdala and hippocampus. The limbic system of the brain can thus be seen as the mediator between our mind (thoughts) and body (physical actions), and vice versa. Without certain biological chemicals we could neither think nor feel (See endnotes on pages 184 and 185).

Impaired thinking may lead to impaired brain chemistry and vice versa. But when it comes to understanding our emotions it is best to make a clear distinction between *sources* and *causes*. There are endless sources over which we can make ourselves depressed, and there are constant chemical imbalances that make us vulnerable to disabling emotive feelings. Yet, in truth, we rarely do so. The reason? We are not mindless robots. A loss or lack of something does not automatically make us depressed, and an overabundance of health and multiple other blessings does not make us automatically happy! Ultimately it is our personal assessment of a fact or event by which we make ourselves happy or sad. But, we dare not overlook the chemical basis of our emotions.

Stressful Messengers in Our Blood

With our mind we can alter the chemistry of our blood. And I don't mean only by choosing to eat or not to eat certain foods, but merely by the way in which we think. It is an interesting and exciting observation that our physical and emotional health is usually under our control. We must be especially alert, however, to the role that excessive stress plays in *most* physical and emotional disorders. And depression is no exception. Over the years I continue to receive reports from both laypersons and professionals that depression is best understood as a multifaceted body-mind-spirit stress disorder.[2]

Whenever our mind attaches some meaningful label to a perception (the apprehension of some sensory input), it becomes an apperception. When we have stressful apperceptions they will be relayed from the cerebral cortex to the limbic system, and, as mentioned before, to the hypothalamus. Here the manufacture of corticotrophin-releasing hormone (CRH/CRF) starts the chain of depression-related chemical events in earnest (see illustration on page 97). It is the CRH produced by the hypothalamus that stimulates the pituitary gland—the so-called master gland of the endocrine system—to respond by manufacturing adrenocorticotropic hormone (ACTH). Please recall, this powerful hormone alerts the adrenal glands to produce, among other substances, the stress-hormone *cortisol*.

Research by Eric Raadsheer (1994) revealed that repeated bouts with depression and its corresponding increases in cortisol levels eventually leads to a loss of neurons in the hippocampus. The latter normally *inhibits* the excessive production of CRH in the hypothalamus. The number of CRH-producing neurons in the hypothalamus is believed to be four times higher in persons with depressive illness than in those who are free of this disorder.

The research findings by Eric Raadsheer seem to confirm my earlier hypothesis (Brandt, 1988) that depression is mainly a stress disorder. Noteworthy in Raadsheer's work is that he is reportedly the first person to demonstrate the existence of visible changes in a part of the human brain (the hippocampus) resulting from the excessive production of cortisol.[3] There are, however, other exciting research studies going on which emphasize other variables, but at this point I remain convinced that excessive mental or physical stress is a key player in depression, and a major contributor to most instances of depressive illness.

The Many Faces of Biochemical Stress

Biochemical stress is a multifaceted phenomenon. Human beings can come to suffer from excessive stress arising from many sources, including poor diet. Biochemical imbalances may result from diets that are low in protein, resulting in low levels of the amino acids tryptophan and tyrosine. A deficiency of tryptophan may result in lowered levels of serotonin, and may also reduce the positive effects of certain antidepressant medications. And the same holds true for tyrosine (which is essential for the neurotransmitters norepinephrine and dopamine).[4] Regrettably, many persons fail to see the link between an unsatisfactory diet and depression. Yet depression is often believed to be associated with nutritional deficiencies.[5] A poor diet, however, although a major stressor, is only one of many potential stressors. Other sources include excessive noise; living in crowded, dangerous, or unsanitary conditions; work pressures, or lack of exercise, recreation, relaxation, sleep, and rest.

Bipolar Disorders: The Other Mood Disorders

Bipolar Disorder, as the name implies, involves two extremes—namely, an episode (or episodes) of excessive euphoria, known as mania, or one or more episodes of mania and/or depression. Thus an individual with a bipolar disorder may have very expansive moods, with or without alternating very low moods. Happily, this person may also experience more balanced moods and can, with proper treatment and a healthy life-style, lead a happy and mostly normal life.

Bipolar Disorder may begin in adolescence or early adulthood and continue throughout life. Excellent treatment, however, is available, and current research is sure to provide even better and more successful treatment. While it is recognized that a bipolar disorder is an illness with perhaps genetic components, this does not mean that treatment should be restricted to medications.

Individuals with a bipolar disorder may greatly benefit from a multi-modal treatment program. This might include not only medications, but also various forms of psychotherapy. Happiness, wellness, and success require a lot more than balancing brain chemistry with medications. A healthy brain first and foremost requires healthy nutrients and healthy thoughts. The latter may be more difficult without some medications, but we must not forget that a mood disorder is a multifaceted problem that requires a multifaceted treatment approach.

Overcoming Depression

The causes of depression are threefold—loss of physical balance, loss of psychological integrity, and loss of spiritual direction. It follows that the treatment for depression is also threefold—physical restoration, emotional reeducation, and spiritual regeneration.[6] Let's look at this.

Physical Restoration

Even if we have only a few symptoms of depression, and especially if we have suicidal thoughts, it is essential to seek professional help without delay. Help is readily available and requires no more than a phone call or visit to a physician, local hospital, or community mental health center. In addition, it is also important to share our concerns with a pastor or a close friend. After obtaining professional help, we still need to do our part as well. Medications are not the sole answer! Here are some suggestions:

Focus on a Healthy Life-style. To overcome depression we must consider a wellness life-style. This may include the formation of some new habits and the elimination of some old ones. We must not be swayed by those who think it is all right to consume alcohol, caffeine, nicotine, or large amounts of refined carbohydrates. Many are or will be paying a high price in needless suffering from the use of these common products.

Because depression often involves an increased need for the neurotransmitter serotonin, there may be a greater affinity for refined carbohydrates—especially products that contain large amounts of sucrose or other sugars. Carbohydrates, especially refined ones such as sugar, promote the uptake of the amino acid tryptophan, which is an important building block for serotonin. The use of refined carbohydrates, however, provide only a temporary respite. It may make us even more susceptible to depression in the long run.

Reduce Sugar Sensitivity. We may suspect low serotonin levels when we have cravings for refined carbohydrates. Consumption of the latter evokes an insulin response from the pancreas to keep blood glucose within acceptable levels. Whenever blood sugar drops too low, however, there will be an emergency call to the adrenal medulla. The response is an outpouring of the energy-producing hormones adrenaline and noradrenaline (epinephrine and norepinephrine). Too many of these stress calls may weaken the adrenal glands and result in problems with low blood sugar, low blood pressure, low body temperature, and low energy levels. This condition highlights, once again, the role of *excessive stress* in the formation of depression. In addition, the stress of the depression itself makes us more vulnerable to hormonal disturbances, creating a vicious cycle.

Our brain uses a lot of glucose. It consumes one-third or more of all the available glucose in the bloodstream. When the glucose level drops too low, the brain suffers with poor memory, mood swings, lack of concentration, and sleeplessness. Low blood sugar is often mainly a dietary problem, but it may also result from illness, overwork, and many other conditions. Sugar sensitivity can be reduced by consuming complex carbohydrates such as whole grain bread and brown rice, rather than refined ones such as white bread and white rice, and eating less of those foods that result in rapidly escalating blood glucose levels as described in the following insert.

The Relationship of Food to Blood Glucose Levels

HIGH	MODERATE	LOW
Beets	Bananas	Apples
Bread (white)	Barley grain	Apricots
Chocolate	Buckwheat	Butter beans
Cookies	Carrots	Cherries
Corn flakes	Kiwi fruit	Fructose[7]
Glucose	Mangoes	Grapefruit
Honey	Oatmeal, regular	Green vegetables
Ice cream	Oranges	Kidney beans
Millet	Peas	Lentils
Parsnips	Pears	Lima beans
Pineapple	Plums	Nuts
Potatoes	Rice (brown)	Onions
Raisins	Shredded wheat	Rye grain
Rice (white)	Sweet potatoes	Tomatoes
Sucrose	Spaghetti	Soybeans
Watermelon	Yams	Whole grains

The information above has been adapted from the so-called Glycemic Index,[8] which identifies some foods that may result in a rapid rise in blood glucose levels, followed by increased insulin responses and lowered blood sugar levels in healthy individuals. Those with sugar sensitivities may respond in more dramatic ways.

To reduce or prevent sugar-induced-mood-swings, consider these suggestions:

- Eat five or six small, balanced meals daily.
- Select mainly foods with low or moderate effects on blood glucose levels, for example: legumes, vegetables, and whole grains.
- Consume high-fiber, and complex carbohydrate foods rather than low-fiber, and refined carbohydrate foods.
- Eat mainly raw foods.
- Never eat junk food.
- Never use alcohol, caffeine, or nicotine.
- Never use refined sugar, or any products with refined sugar.
- Never use any artificial sweeteners.
- Never overeat.

Note: *Always obtain medical advice before changing your diet.*

There are additional helpful steps important to physical restoration, and good physical and mental health, which are described at the end of the next chapter.

Emotional Re-Education

Ultimately only a change in thinking will change our feelings. Although there are many variables involved, we must not lose sight of the central theme in this book—that God has given most of us the opportunity to wisely choose our thoughts, feelings, and actions. Emotional reeducation focuses primarily on identifying and correcting errors in our thoughts and beliefs such as "allness thinking." Here are some examples:

"I am always left out."
"I am never appreciated."
"I will never be happy."
"Things will never change."
"I don't have any happy memories."

"I will always be alone."
"Everybody is better off than I am."
"Nothing ever goes right for me."

Catchwords to use with caution are *always, never, any, all, everybody, constantly, nothing, no one*, and so forth. It is highly unlikely that someone is always left out, never appreciated, or does not have any happy memories. There are, of course, many other self-defeating cognitions that result in serious misinterpretations, misunderstandings, and unhappiness. Among them are: jumping to conclusions, labeling, hasty generalizations, judging or categorizing individuals, and various forms of arrogance, slander, bias, ignorance, intolerance and prejudice. We must stay alert to the fact that "The tongue has the power of life and death." (Prov. 18:21), and that "A word aptly spoken is like apples of gold in settings of silver" (Prov. 25:11). As Christians we must make sure that what we say—to ourselves and to others—is based on truth, reason, faith and love. To ensure that our thoughts are increasingly of the wholesome variety, we must challenge those thoughts that result in unwanted emotions and actions.

Spiritual Regeneration
Whatever the source of our depression, whether physical, emotional, or spiritual, we are created in God's image and we must look to God for help and reorientation. Take the promises of God seriously and fully believe that He will "give good gifts to those who ask him" (Matt. 7:11).

There is a misunderstanding among some Christians that depression is in the will of God. This is what I have said earlier on this subject: "It is true that nothing in human life falls outside the sphere of God's will, but that is not the same as saying that God is equally the cause of good and evil in human life. Such a statement would be blasphemous. It would confuse God the Father with Satan the father of lies. No: God is the fountainhead of all that is good!" (Brandt, 1988).

Throughout the Scriptures we find confirmation that God allies Himself with believers in the battle against depression. Believers are not robots, nor victims of forces beyond their control. Believers have been graced with choice, accountability, and responsibility. They are participators, not spectators. Every believer is challenged by God to make wise choices and stick to commitments. Since depression is clearly not a part of God's will for us and since He wants us to have victory over depression, we need to be mindful of the many Scriptures that spell out the blessings that God wants us to enjoy. Consider just a few:

- Victory over the world (1 John 4:4)
- Joy in various trials (1 Pet. 1:6)
- Freedom from despair in the midst of perplexity (2 Cor. 4:8)
- Rest from our burdens (Matt. 11:28)
- Courage in the face of opposition (Ps. 56:3, 4)
- Renewal of the mind and a transformed life (Rom. 12:1, 2)
- The enjoyment of wholesome emotions (Eph. 4:31, 32)
- Control over our spirit (Prov. 25:28)
- Good health (3 John 2)
- Soundness in body, mind, and spirit (1 Thess. 5:23)
- Peace (John 14:27)

Spiritual regeneration requires that we look above and beyond our human limitations. This, in turn, helps us to identify and remove a possible God-void, God-neglect, or God-confusion. Ultimately this means that we must decide for eternal life, reconciliation, and victory. Here is a brief description of how we can do this.

Decide for Eternal Life. God-void depression results from not knowing that it is the will of God that we are to be saved by the blood of Christ. Following our own imperfect will and believing in godless materialistic humanism, inevitably leads to disillusionment. The answer to God-void depression is the yielding of our own imperfect will to the perfect will of God. We must repent of our sins, and believe in and call on the name of Jesus. To discern the will of God, it is helpful to read the following Scriptures:

Deuteronomy 30:19, 20; John 3:16, 3:36; 5:24; 6:47; Matthew 6:33; Romans 10:9; and 1 John 2:17. Then we must make a decision for eternal life! A decision to invite God to fill the void.

Decide for Reconciliation. God-neglect depression results from turning our back on fellowship with God. Following our own imperfect will in disobedience to God's perfect will inevitably leads to guilt, among other things. The answer to God-neglect depression is repentance and deciding to wholeheartedly walk with God again. This includes loving Him and others selflessly, forgiving others, being witnesses for Christ, bearing good fruit, and increasing in knowledge, understanding, and wisdom. To discern the will of God for reconciliation it is helpful to read Scriptures such as: Psalm 24:3–4; Matthew 5:48; 18:11; Luke 15:3–32; Romans 6:1; 1 Thessalonians 4:3–7; Hebrews 12:14; 1 John 3:3-10; 5:18. Having done this, we must decide to wholeheartedly walk with God in complete surrender to His will.

Decide for Victory. God-confusion depression results from loss of spiritual discernment, which may also be reflected in doubt, fear, or worry. Following our own imperfect will inevitably leads to a loss of clarity and vision. The answer to God-confusion depression is to steadfastly claim victory by holding onto the Word of God. God promises us total victory over all our troubles. To more fully discern the will of God for our lives, and realizing that confusion is not of Him, it is helpful to read: Psalm 18:28–32; Isaiah 54:17; John 14:1; Romans 8:15, 16, 37; 1 Corinthians 6:11; 2 Corinthians 4:8–10; 2 Timothy 4:18; Titus 3:5; and 2 Peter 5:7. Having read these Scriptures we must now remove all confusion by focusing on the Word of God.

9

Overcomers Lead Happier Lives

Our emotions are the outcome of our perceptions and thoughts. As long as these are realistically, rationally, and positively integrated, we will not suffer from emotional disturbances or prolonged unhappiness. This holds true even if we are living under stressful conditions. The key to emotional control is to understand how specific thinking leads to specific feelings. If we are not happy with our feelings we must first change our thinking. This chapter explains how emotional control helps overcomers to have happier lives. The chapter ends with a reminder that a healthy mind requires a healthy body.

Generally speaking, we first think, then feel and act. Whether we feel sad or happy, angry or calm, depressed or elated—whatever our emotional state—it is the final outcome of our thinking. Even in case of deep grief, a state of shock, a sense of despair over the death of a loved one, or the end of a vital relationship, we can only overcome these painful feelings by changing our thinking.

Thoughts Before Feelings

Simply put, whenever we perceive something we also tell ourselves something about that perception. Our past experiences, beliefs, attitudes, and so forth, are all ingredients in our perceptions. We perceive what we are prepared to perceive. It was a commander of a Roman army who said, "I came, I saw, I conquered." What he saw was not just a grandly panoramic landscape but a territory that he believed could be overpowered. When a lumberman walks into a pine forest, he sees not only an impressive stand of tall, straight evergreens; what he sees is timber that will yield thousands of board feet of lumber. A child watching her father on a tractor pulling out a large stump in the front yard, on seeing the hole that is left behind, may cry out, "Look, daddy, a sandbox!" Our perceptions are loaded with insights and thoughts arising from our "worldview," and yield a corresponding set of feelings.

It is a revelation for some individuals to discover that the way in which they perceive and think determines how they feel. A revelation it is, but it is rooted in the fact that the thinking portion of our brain sends signals to the feeling portion of our brain. Those actions that seem completely automatic or spontaneous usually reflect attitudes, which are the final outcome of our well-learned beliefs. When these beliefs are false, based on misinterpretations or misapprehensions, the resulting emotional damage can be considerable.

Feelings Before Thoughts?

I have explained that, in general, we first think, then feel and act. And that is true. Nevertheless, there are times when we may experience an immediate emotional reaction to an auditory or a visual perception. These are usually of an emergency nature. Normally, our emotional reactions or responses are handled by various parts of the limbic system and other parts of the brain: the hypothalamus, thalamus, and cerebral cortex.[1] Neurological sensory pathways notify the thalamus of whatever is going on internally or externally before the thalamus sends a message to the cortex (thinking portion of the brain), where it is interpreted for action and then relayed to the amygdala. But, what if we are suddenly faced with a life or death situation and need an instant emotional reaction? In that case, there is an emotional equivalent to the so-called mind-body fight or flight response.

Neuroscientist Joseph LeDoux (Goleman, 1995) found that emergency emotional and other instantaneous emotional reactions can take place without sensory inputs going first from the thalamus to the neocortex and from there to the amygdala for interpretation and action.

LeDoux found a small bundle of neurons that provide a direct connection between the thalamus and the amygdala. How significant is this? Goleman (1995) explains what happens if some significant event is captured by our eye:

> A visual signal first goes from the retina to the thalamus, where it is translated into the language of the brain. Most of the message then goes to the visual cortex, where it is analyzed and assessed for meaning and appropriate response; if that response is emotional, a signal goes to the amygdala to activate the emotional centers. But a smaller portion of the original signal goes straight from the thalamus to the amygdala in a quicker transmission, allowing a faster (though less precise) response.

We Must Think Right to Feel Right!

When we learn that the thinking portion of the brain is not always immediately involved in the creation of an emotional event, we do well to make a distinction between *reaction* and *response*. When an auditory or visual signal goes straight to the feeling portion of the brain, we are dealing with very limited automatic reactions. Also, we need to be mindful that the actual time difference between a direct emotional reaction and indirect emotional response may only be a *small fraction of a second*. In emergencies that is wonderful, as it can make a difference between life and death. But when it comes to our day-to-day emotive feelings (happy or unhappy ones), the thinking portion of the brain remains the most important player.

The role of the amygdala, however, is very important. For the *amygdala* plays a crucial role in *storing emotional reactions* to past events. The amygdala works in conjunction with yet another part of our brain's limbic system, namely the *hippocampus*. The latter *stores memories* and thus helps provide the context of meaning to our emotional reactions and responses.[2]

As we consider findings in neuroscience, we are also reminded that all-too-often our immediate emotional reactions are incorrect ones. When devoid of constructive thinking, they may well be dangerous, or otherwise dysfunctional. Clearly, if the amygdala was our only guide, and we only used emotional reactions, we might find ourselves quite often in trouble. But there is a solution to all of this. Let's have a look.

Self-Talk! Self-Talk! Self-Talk!

Happily, the solution is not terribly complex. Contrary to popular opinion, it is possible to create more positive emotions once we learn to have more objective perceptions, and more so-lution-focused self-talk. Bible-readers will readily recognize the role of self-talk in creating a better outlook on life. The psalmists were especially good at it: "Why are you downcast, O my soul? Why so disturbed within me?" asked one of them (Ps. 42:5, 11; 43:5). "Praise the LORD, O my soul; all my inmost being, praise his holy name," sang another (Ps. 103:1). Self-talk lies at the heart of this discussion. Simply stated: negative emotive feelings are the result of negative thinking, and positive emotive feelings are the result of positive thinking.

For a wholesome life—a life grounded in truth, reason, and faith—we need *wholesome* self-talk. When practiced regularly, this will bring us a happier and more peaceful life. To check on our self-talk, we need to repeat the three questions mentioned in an earlier chapter: (1) Is it *realistic?* (factual, truthful?), (2) Is it *rational?* (life-enhancing, goal-achieving?), (3) Is it *positive?* (love-based, faith-based?). The self-talk of a Christian overcomer must line up with truth, reason, and faith. If our self-talk is rooted in the reality of the Word and will of God, it will result in feelings of contentment, joy, and peace. How we talk makes *all* the difference in how we feel.

Self-Talk Makes All the Difference?

Indeed, but it had better be wholesome self-talk! One way to learn more about wholesome self-talk is to consider several employees who work for the same employer, under exactly the same conditions; yet, remarkably, they all react differently and consequently feel differently. The difference is their self-talk, and that makes *all* the difference. One person becomes angry, another anxious, another feels guilty, and still another becomes depressed. Let's take the time to sharpen our insights by considering the story of the following four employees (Brandt, 1988):

The Angry Employee

Unchallenged Events[3]

Perception: My boss constantly criticizes me by calling me stupid.

Self-Talk: He is a real jerk. He has no people skills at all. He is not fit to be a boss. I hate him.

Emotion: I feel angry.

Challenged Events

Perception: My boss constantly criticizes me by calling me stupid.

Self-Talk: Yes, he calls me stupid but I know that he calls other employees by other unflattering names. Anyway, his calling me stupid does not make me stupid, anymore than his calling me a rhino would make me a rhino. True, he has few people skills, but he is not really a jerk—just an unhappy person. And doing what he is doing is the natural outcome of his mental outlook, his thinking. Unless he changes his thinking he will continue to act as he does.

Emotion: I feel calm

Mental Practice/Self-Talk Script

I am sitting at my desk when my boss drops in to look at my work. A second later he calls me stupid but I am prepared. I shunt aside my resentment, remind myself that he has a serious weakness, and silently pray for him. I remind myself that, while I do make mistakes, I am an experienced employee and highly valued by the company. Regardless of what my boss says to me, I am still free to think my own constructive thoughts and feel composed and happy.

The Anxious Employee

Unchallenged Events

Perception: My boss constantly criticizes me by calling me stupid.

Self-Talk: This really scares me. Every time he comes to my desk I feel my heart race. One of these days I will be fired.

Emotion: I feel anxious.

Challenged Events

Perception: My boss constantly criticizes me by calling me stupid.

Self-Talk: My boss does criticize me, but I am no exception. He does it to the other employees as well. I will be upset only if I make myself upset. Nothing is going to get worse unless I allow it to happen. Basically, I am not afraid of him. I have no reason to be. He has not done me any physical harm and I will not be dismissed. This situation has gone on for several years. Even if I was dismissed, that would not be the end of the world. I would not starve. My boss is basically not a tyrant out to destroy me. He has some seriously self-defeating habits. Actually he is very lonely and insecure and probably more anxious than I have been.

Emotion: I feel calm.

Mental Practice/Self-Talk Script

I have made an error and my boss calls me into his office. As I am walking to his office, I think about the wonderful opportunity I have to bless my boss by my willingness to act rather than react. I can hear myself say, "I am sorry about the error, and I will correct it immediately. Thank you for telling me, and I am grateful for all your help." I feel calm and good while I am doing this. I notice that I am speaking slowly, while looking directly at his face. It is good to know that there are no inferior or superior people, but only imperfect ones. I am happy for this opportunity to grow, and I praise God for this. I feel calm and happy.

The Guilty Employee
Unchallenged Events

Perception: My boss constantly criticizes me by calling me stupid.

Self-Talk: I realize that I need to shape up. I make far too many errors, and I don't seem to be able to learn from my mistakes. I am not taking things seriously enough. I ought to be grateful for my job and work harder at pleasing my boss. Also, I shouldn't have talked back the last time. I had no right to do that. It's my fault that no one likes me. I am pretty bad and hard to get along with.

Emotion: I feel *guilty.*

Challenged Events

Perception: My boss constantly criticizes me by calling me stupid.

Self-Talk: It is not true that my boss criticizes me constantly. This would mean that he does it all the time. Actually, this only happens a few times a week. He is in the habit of calling anyone stupid who makes a mistake. I think it is just a habit that he has picked up somewhere. He may not even be aware that he does this, and no one may have bothered to point this out to him. I can do my best to make fewer errors, but in this kind of work it is common to make some mistakes. We are all working under tremendous pressures with deadlines to meet every day. I do learn from my mistakes, and rarely make the same mistake twice. Also, I take things seriously and I am happy to have a job. If I talked back, then I should have, for the world is an orderly place, and our actions are the result of our thoughts. This means that

117

they are the logical outcome of our beliefs, attitudes, and opinions. Only if I change my self-talk will my feelings and actions change. It is nonsense that no one likes me; for one thing, my spouse and children love me, and I have many friends. I am not bad because I make some mistakes, and I would not be human if I did not make any mistakes at all.

Emotion: I feel calm.

Mental Practice/Self-Talk Script

I am listening to my boss calling me stupid but I am not allowing his words to sink in and hurt me. I focus on the overall situation, not on his words. Did I really make an error? In what way can I do a better job and help my boss? The more he screams, the more convinced I become that self-control is important. I remind myself of the Scripture in Proverbs 25:28 that says: "Like a city whose walls are broken down, is a man who lacks self-control." I feel good and happy doing that. I am taking the opportunity to learn from the lack of emotional control of my boss, so that I can strengthen my own and set a good example. Each incident now becomes a blessing rather than a curse.

The Depressed Employee
Unchallenged Events

Perception: My boss constantly criticizes me by calling me stupid.

Self-talk: I continue to make all kinds of mistakes. It is no wonder that no one likes me. I should be far more qualified than I am, but I cannot learn very well. I should be more careful, but I cannot change. I see no purpose in staying on this job for I never do anything right anyway. I am a real failure—a born loser. I lack willpower to stick to things. I hate myself for it. When I get up in the morning, I feel depressed just thinking about getting to work. I have more and more difficulties in getting to sleep or staying asleep. I dislike my job and I dislike myself. I am physically and mentally tired. I have started to lose weight. I feel sorry for myself being in this terrible situation. I doubt that it will change. I am sorry that I am so stupid. I should be more qualified and intelligent. Life is a real bummer.

Emotion: I feel depressed.

Challenged Events

Perception: My boss constantly criticizes me by calling me stupid.

Self-Talk: It is true that my boss sometimes calls me stupid. However, this does not happen every day. I do make mistakes, but I have learned to make fewer mistakes. I have checked on the error rates of the other employees and they are about the same as mine. This means that I am just as qualified as anyone else in my department. I have a number of very good friends, and obviously I can only be as qualified as I am now. Saying that I should be more qualified without additional training and experience is pure nonsense. In addition, I have all the qualifications the job calls for. I have received four promotions since I started this job five years ago. All my effectiveness reports show that I am a qualified and respected employee. I believe that I have gotten in a worse habit than my boss. He calls me stupid, and probably does not mean it. I call myself stupid—knowing that I am not—and have begun to believe it. It makes a difference what I call myself. I am a child of God. I am respected, accepted, and understood by God. God loves me. I know that my physical symptoms are directly related to my thinking about the job, because during weekends and vacations I feel so much better. I have changed in many ways, and with the help of God I can change completely. I am mindful of the Scripture that says, "I can do everything through him, who gives me strength" (Phil. 4:13).

Emotion: I feel calm.

Mental Practice/Self-Talk Script

My boss walks up to me and calls me stupid, but I am prepared. I immediately have a wonderful sense of tranquillity come over me. In my mind I am silently saying, "Thank you, Lord, for the peace you bring into my heart," and as I listen to my boss I do not react negatively, but correct the things that he wants to correct. I also see myself looking at him with the love of God, and I hear myself saying, "I will be happy to correct these errors. Thank you for bringing them to my attention." I praise and thank God for every opportunity that comes my way to increase my faith in Him and to share His love in a practical way.

The four employees we have just discussed were all working in the same office for the same employer and were treated in an identical manner. Yet they did not react or feel the same. Their varied reactions of *anger, anxiety, guilt,* and *depression* were directly related to their self-talk, and the removal of their negative emotive feelings was the direct result of their challenged self-talk. This is something that we can do either verbally or in writing.

Errors in our Thinking

At this juncture, it is good to take a close look at some of the common thinking errors that may have intruded into our lives. Some of these thinking errors (for example, catastrophizing, magnification, and mind reading) are probably more familiar than others (for example, consensus attribution, or negative memory bias). Whatever the case may be, it is important to become thoroughly familiar with these common thinking errors, and to realize that they are only the "tip of the iceberg."[4]

Common Thinking Errors and Misbeliefs

	Thinking Errors	*Unchallenged Beliefs*	*Challenged Beliefs*
Arbitrary Inference	Drawing conclusions, or making decisions in the absence of sufficient evidence.	"I will be a bum for the rest of my life if I fail this course."	"Failing this course has nothing to do with being a bum."
Biased Attribution	Assuming that other people say and do things only because of ulterior motives.	"She is only friendly to me so that I will give in to her demands."	"It is not a good idea to second guess that her friendliness is self-serving."
Catastrophizing	Overemphasizing a worst possible scenario.	"The plane is overdue—it has crashed and no one survived."	"The plane is overdue and perhaps there is a problem."
Consensus Misattribution	Overestimating the number of people who think, feel or act as we do.	"All the people in this country support my beliefs."	"Many people seem to support my beliefs."
Dichotomous Thinking	All or nothing 'absolutistic' thinking.	"I failed to fix the noise in my car I am worthless."	"I am glad that I tried to fix my car, even if I did not succeed."
Emotional Reasoning	Erroneously equating subjective feelings with objective reality.	"I feel that I will never succeed."	"Sometimes I think that I will not succeed."

121

Common Thinking Errors and Misbeliefs

	Thinking Errors	Unchallenged Beliefs	Challenged Beliefs
Fortune Telling	Assuming human beings can or should know exactly what the future holds.	"I should have known that an investment with Meteoric Climb would have made me rich."	"If I had known that Meteoric Climb would bring such great returns I would have invested."
Magnification	Greatly overestimating the significance of a fact or event.	"I was late for dinner twice this week; it will ruin my marriage."	"I was late for dinner twice, but I scheduled my work better, and I have explained this to my spouse."
Mind Reading	Elevating *guessing* to supernaturally *knowing* what others are thinking.	"I know what he is thinking about me."	"I don't know what he is thinking unless he tells me."
Minimization	Greatly understating the significance of a fact or event.	"Anyone could have made millions selling brushes."	"Someone else might also have succeeded in this business."
Negative Memory Bias	Habitually remembering negative rather than positive experiences.	"All I can remember about my career is that I was never really in charge."	"Many opportunities came with my career, even though I was never in charge."
Overgeneralization	Making sweeping conclusions based on scanty data.	"I failed to see the significance of *perestroika*, and will never be a political scientist."	"As a fallible person it is easy to miss the significance of any event."

Unless our thinking is realistic, rational, and positive, we may come to suffer from much unhappiness. Since feelings flow from thinking it is often important to challenge our self-talk and remove unrealistic, irrational, and/or negative thoughts and beliefs. To ensure that our newly formed wholesome self-talk becomes more permanent, we can create self-talk scripts similar to the ones described in this chapter. It is helpful to memorize such a script, and then to mentally rehearse it a few times a day. Mental practice, with a *wholesome* self-talk script, is a safe and efficient way to overcome negative emotions, unwanted habits, and other forms of self-defeating behavior. Prayerfully entered into, this aspect of the renewal of our mind brings glory to God, honors Christ, yields inner peace, and is entirely in keeping with Scripture (Rom. 12:2).

A Healthy Mind Needs Healthy Nutrients

In *The Renewed Mind* (Brandt, 1999), as well as in other books and various seminars over the past twenty years, I have provided a brief outline of a *modified* wellness diet. I have always received positive comments on that diet, but more recently—as a result of conducting a six-month health awareness project (The Maple Ridge Rural Health Awareness Project)—I am forced to conclude that there is only limited value in a *modified* wellness diet. I now more fully realize that to effectively combat chronic illness, unnecessary suffering, and premature death, we need to be *committed* to a 100% healthy diet as the foundation of a 100% healthy life-style. We may call this diet the Genesis Diet (see Genesis 1:29).

Even the Genesis Diet, however, is not a cure-all for every physical or emotional problem, nor is this diet possible at all times for all people. The body and mind are influenced by many variables, including: attitude; genetics; education; personality; environmental factors (such as climate, pollution, and the availability of food supplies); relationships; and, life-style habits such as recreation and exercise.

It must also be remembered, however, that dietary changes— especially for those who are frail, pregnant, or ill—must be made under competent medical supervision; tailored to the particular physical and mental condition of an individual; at times gradually implemented; evaluated in conjunction with other health-promoting steps, such as exercise, fasting, or colon cleansing; and, designed within the environmental and logistical resources of an individual. Cutting back on some dangerous health practices, or following a so-called "transition diet" might be recommended as a first step on the road to wellness. For many this is not an easy road. Nevertheless, I remain firmly convinced that the foundation of good physical *and* mental health is found, first and foremost, in a healthy diet. An optimally functioning mind—a mind that can choose and decide wisely—is simply not possible without an optimally functioning brain.

A truly healthy diet, I now believe, is God's original diet described in Genesis 1:29. This diet was free of all animal products. Animal products are neither good for us, nor necessary—in spite of all we have been taught since childhood, and the hundreds of millions of advertising dollars that are spend every year to reinforce those erroneous childhood teachings. Study after study, for example, makes it abundantly clear that meat and dairy products are *bad* for our health. And there are many other things—such as tap water, soft drinks, alcohol, caffeine, refined carbohydrates (e.g. sugar), or hydrogenated fats—that have no place in any wellness diet. The Genesis Diet, in my opinion, can both prevent and combat most of our illnesses. *A modern Genesis diet is free of all junk food, and all addictive substances, and consists mainly* (about 75%) *of raw fruits and vegetables, wholegrains, nuts, seeds, legumes, healthy oils, distilled water, and fresh vegetable juices.*[5]

A major mistake made by many mental health professionals is to overlook the obvious fact that a healthy brain requires a steady flow of non-allergenic, healthy nutrients. Unhealthy nutrients, insufficient nutrients, allergenic substances, as well as other variables (e.g. highly glycemic nutrients), may negatively impact the brain, and hence, the mind. There is no anxiety disorder, mood disorder, personality disorder, or *any* other mental disorder, that is not influenced to some extent by nutrition and life-style. To overlook the importance of healthy nutrition and a healthy life-style for the optimal functioning of a healthy person is folly. To overlook that need in those with physical or mental/emotional problems is disastrous.

While nutrition may play only a minor role in some mental disorders (e.g. personality disorders), it may play a major role in others (e.g. anxiety or mood disorders). Every mental/emotional problem will benefit from a healthy diet and healthy life-style, especially one free from addictive substances such as alcohol, caffeine, nicotine, and sugar. Having stressed the importance of a healthy life-style, I would also like to stress that each individual is *unique* and that there are some individuals whose specific situation calls for a different approach than the one described in this section.

Over the years I have learned that emotional problems are often intertwined with personality styles and lifestyles, and in particular with dietary practices. I have also learned that psychotherapy is often less effective, and sometimes contraindicated, unless the mind is blessed with a well-fed, well-shielded, and well-stimulated brain. Such a brain needs, among other things: sufficient oxygen; steady glucose levels; balanced electrolyte levels; specific vitamins, amino acids, and fatty acids; shielding from allergenic and toxic substances; sufficient sleep; and varied sensory stimulation.

Emotional problems are sometimes intertwined with brain allergies, low blood sugar, and/or toxic problems. Frequently identified allergenic foods are beef, chicken, citrus, corn, dairy, eggs, pork, shellfish, soy, sugar, wheat, and yeast. Allergic reactions may result in a variety of physical as well as emotional problems.

A Brief Summary

In this chapter we have looked at *the anatomy of emotions* (we first perceive and think, then feel), *the importance of wholesome self-talk* (truth, reason, and faith), and *the integration of body, brain, and mind* (we need a healthy diet and life-style as well as healthy cognitions). Overcomers, however, do not live in a vacuum. They must deal with far more than just themselves—they must also deal with their *social* and *spiritual* environment. The next chapter takes a look at what else it takes to survive in an "age of folly."

Quotes to Ponder, 1949–1999

"My interpretation of NATURAL FOODS is that food which is nourishing by virtue of the presence of organic life in it. In this category I place all raw vegetables and fruits and their fresh, raw, unprocessed juices, and nuts." Dr. N. W. Walker, *Become Younger,* Norwalk Press, 1949.

"Dr. McCormick of Toronto, in Medical Record of September, 1947, shows us how infectious diseases have been becoming less and less prevalent in the last hundred years, thanks, he believes, entirely to better distribution of *fresh fruits and vegetables."* Dr. Leon DeSeblo, *Sickness and Senility Are Unnecessary,* Health Research, Mokelumne Hill, CA, 1951.

"The medical world has been looking for a remedy to cure disease, notwithstanding the obvious fact that nature needs no remedy—she needs only an opportunity to exercise her own prerogative of self-healing." J. H. Tilden, M. D., *Toxemia Explained,* Health Research, Mokelumne Hill, CA, 1952.

"Until there is a general understanding of high-level natural health, I believe the alarming growth of cancer, and all other degenerative forms of disease, must continue." James C. Thomson, *Nature Cure From the Inside: The Why of Chronic Disease,* Kingston Clinic, Edinburgh, 1953.

"Those people who choose to live on a *raw food diet* should include *baked potato* and *some form of cooked grain* such as brown rice, buckwheat, millet, whole wheat, or oatmeal, in order not to starve their bodies of the B vitamins. The B vitamins are found in these grain foods. These are the vitamins that are not destroyed by cooking, aging or staleness. Vitamins A, C, and D, and minerals besides, are found in the raw fruits and vegetables. It is for this reason that raw foods should be consumed in high daily rations." Alice Chase, M.D., Parker Publishing Company, Inc., West Nyack, NY, 1954.

"Most people have come to think of the grains as the 'staff of life.' The truth is that the greens are the real 'staff of life' and that the grains can be regarded at best as a poor second." Dr. Max Warmbrand, *Here's Health . . . Nature's Way,* Pyramid Books, 1962.

"Only with the help of God can any person be his very best, for we are all powerless in our own strength and wisdom to combat those opposing forces which are constantly at work to hinder our progress." Richard E. Hunton, M. D., *Formula for Fitness,* Fleming H. Revell Company, Westwood, NJ, 1966.

"The average sugar consumption in this country today is eleven times as much as it was in 1900, and it is still going up year by year, because the craving for it is like taking drugs. It may get so high one day, and low blood sugar may become so prevalent, that people will be shot down in the streets like dogs by sugar-crazed people. No one will be safe!" J. I. Rodale, *Natural Health, Sugar and the Criminal Mind,* Pyramid Books, New York, 1968.

"That I, a physician, began the consumption of exclusively raw vegetables and fruit was a consequence of a personal illness, a case of cancer of the breast." Dr. Kristine Nolfi, *My Experiences With Living Foods,* The Provoker Press, 1970.

"I eat all raw, fresh fruits and vegetables, but no dried fruits, and no canned fruits or vegetables." Rydie Mae, *How I Conquered Cancer Naturally,* Production House, 1975.

"It is claimed by the best authorities that the human body has the ability to repair itself, to construct and reconstruct its cellular structure over and over again, if the proper nutrients are provided . . . I plead with you to give a total raw juice and raw food diet an unimpeded chance for 10 short days. What you feel and see will give you the encouragement you need to continue. You, and you alone, hold your fate in your hands." John R. Tobe, *The Miracles of Live Juices and Raw Foods,* Provoker Press, St. Catharines, Ontario, 1977.

"Strong evidence is emerging that such diverse mental and emotional conditions as schizophrenia, manic depression, anxiety, and uncontrolled aggression are primarily chemical in origin—the results of allergic reactions to food or pollutants, deficiencies in the body of one or more trace minerals, toxic poisoning from heavy metals such as lead or combinations of all three." Richard Mackarness, M. D., *Chemical Victims,* Pan Books Ltd, London, 1980.

"Sugar consumption in the USA has increased by over 1000 percent since 1821. It has been noted that degenerative diseases, metabolic disorders, and such things as antisocial behavior have also dramatically increased. Many experts suspect a direct relationship between the rise in ill health and the use of sugar." Frans M. J. Brandt, EdD, ABMP, *The Way to Wholeness,* Crossway Books, Westchester, IL, 1984.

"Clearly our original diet was vegetarian (Gen. 1:29), and this did not change until after the flood had destroyed the earth's vegetation. It was only then that God gave permission to use flesh foods. . . . The Bible is as up-to-date as ever, for we are increasingly learning that meat is not good for us and that animal fat is very unhealthy. Green vegetables (herbs) and fruits, on the other hand, are among the healthiest foods on earth." Frans M. J. Brandt, EdD, ABMP *Victory Over Depression,* Baker Book House, 1988.

"Besides the life-threatening cancers, circulatory diseases (heart attacks, stroke, high blood pressure, etc.), and diabetes that are closely tied to our typical diet, our society is ravaged by the less threatening but painful problems of headaches, allergies, skin problems, arthritis, respiratory problems, osteoporosis and bone fractures, obesity, hypoglycemia, and tooth decay. These maladies are among a host that are closely linked to the kinds of foods we feed ourselves." *Healthy Habits,* David and Anne Frähm, Pinon Press, Colorado Springs, CO, 1993.

"My conclusion after all these years of research and experience is that WE DO NOT HAVE TO BE SICK!!! Disease and sickness are self-inflicted. Almost every physical problem, other than accidents, is *caused* by improper diet and lifestyle! All we have to do to be well is eat and live according to the way God intended!" Dr. George H. Malkmus, *God's Way to Ultimate Health,* Hallelujah Acres Publishing, Shelby, NC, 1995.

"I must admit that making the switch to a vegetarian diet took some doing. I'd be lying if I said it was easy." Anne E. Frähm, *A Cancer Battle Plan,* Tarcher/ Putnam Books, 1997.

"A sip of milk contains hundreds of different substances, each one having the potential to exert a powerful biological effect when taken independently of the others. Proteins and hormones, fat and cholesterol, pesticides with vitamin D added, viruses and bacteria . . . all combine to produce a vast array of ailments in our society." Robert Cohen, *Milk—The Deadly Poison,* Argus Publishing, Englewood Cliffs, NJ, 1998.

"Caffeine raises homocysteine levels (which is related to heart disease) in two ways. We know that the elimination of homocysteine from the blood requires optimal amounts of folic acid, vitamin B-12, and vitamin B-6. Caffeine depletes these vital nutrients. Secondly, caffeine appears to interfere with the normal breakdown of homocysteine." Stephen Cherniske, M.S., *Caffeine Blues,* Warner Books, NY, 1998.

"We must do all we can to prevent the destruction of our health. This includes staying away from such health hazards as junk food, addictive substances, a sedentary lifestyle, unnecessary medications, illegal substances, environmental pollutants (such as neurotoxic agents and carcinogens), excessive stress, violent 'sports,' reckless driving, and work addiction." Frans M. J. Brandt, EdD, ABMP, *The Renewed Mind,* Winepress Publishing, Mukilteo, WA 1999.

Part Four:

The Discernment
of Overcomers

10

OVERCOMERS ARE ALERT SURVIVORS IN AN AGE OF FOLLY

We are living in an Age of Folly in which masses of people have unmistakably lost their grip on reality. They are centered in their own subjectivity and guided by nothing more than shallow opinions. In their wretchedness they neglect the great traditions of wisdom and seek out teachers who, while conveying an air of wisdom, not infrequently take advantage of them. The history of human folly is simply being reenacted over and over. To survive in the present Age of Folly, Christian overcomers must maintain a firm grip on wisdom—wisdom rooted in the reality of the Word and will of God.

The media seem to thrive on the depiction of the absurd follies people engage in, while doing next to nothing to detail the unsensational ways in which human beings can become wise. Obviously, it takes no great effort to act foolish. The challenge for us is to become persons who act, speak, and think wisely. So where is the trail that leads from folly to wisdom?

For centuries now Christian believers, having experienced the immense potential for folly and disaster in their own life and the lives of others, have found Scripture to be a great corrective, an inexhaustible fountain of wisdom. As Frederick Buechner, a Christian minister and novelist, once pointed out:

> So many people think of the Bible as primarily a source of moral truth, a book of arbitrary and hopelessly outmoded rules of what is right conduct and what is wrong conduct morally conceived. But surely the Bible is not first of all a book of moral truth. I would call it instead a book of truth about the way life is. These strange old Scriptures present life as having been ordered in a certain way, with certain laws as inextricably built into it as the law of gravity is built into the physical universe (*The Hungering Dark*, 1981).

The quotation from Buechner points in the right direction: "Wisdom is a reality-based phenomenon" (Plantinga Jr., 1995). It is fundamental knowledge about the way things really are and insight into how that knowledge can be turned to one's advantage. In Scripture such wisdom books as Proverbs and the Letter of James clearly indicate what to look for. James speaks of "the wisdom that comes from heaven" (3:17). It is indeed from heaven, for it presupposes the law and the gospel. But it deals with things below, the things under our very noses—the things that puzzle and imprison us. Nothing is more realistic.

Wisdom can also be described as the diligent practice of tracing the patterns the Creator has woven into the fabric of the world. *To be wise is to know that God's creation is rooted in His will, structured by His wisdom, and directed toward His goals, and to conduct oneself accordingly. Consequently, in the Christian view anyone who ignores that will, that wisdom, and those goals is a fool.* It is the nature of folly to run one's life against the grain of the universe and to overlook reality. It is the nature of folly to be unaccommodating to the will of God. It is the nature of folly to "saw off the branch one is sitting on," to "shoot oneself in the foot," to ignore the causes of ones own downfall.

It cannot be stated clearly enough and often enough that "the fear of the Lord"—the dreadful love for the designer and manager of the universe—is the beginning of wisdom (Prov. 1:7; 9:10; Ps.

111:10). It is critical to living human life. Just as at one time the fear of Pharaoh was essential to getting along in Pharaoh's Egypt and Pharaoh's court, so the fear of the Lord is a prerequisite to getting along in His world. There is reason to fear: God is good, but He is not safe (C. S. Lewis). This fear is characterized by alertness—loving attentiveness—to who He is and to what He looks for. Only a fool would describe a meeting with God as "fun" (Plantinga Jr., 1995).

The world God created was made to work well. It is rationally constructed. The appointed means are well adapted to established ends. While we may be "out of line" and "out of order," the creation is hardly a chaos. Such chaos as seems to exist still functions under the daily supervision of a wise Creator. The wise person is one who discerns the interconnectedness of all things under God's control, while fools ignore it, dreaming in their arrogance that they can get away with it. *So fools go on wanting wealth without working, wanting a clean environment while trashing it, wanting a harvest of peace without sowing the righteousness that makes for peace, wanting good neighbors without being a good neighbor, wanting good government without being good citizens.* They go on wanting the impossible, until the bubble bursts. Such folly is the child of pride, the refusal to be subject to the way things are in the world.

The Lineage of Pride

Pride, the root cause of all things "out of line," has a long history. According to Scripture, it first developed in an angel of "transcendent brightness" (Isa. 14:12–15). Though no privilege was denied him, he could not stand being only a brilliant member of the heavenly choirs, but wanted to hold the baton of the Supreme Conductor himself. So he was cast out, sentenced to "bottomless perdition" where there was only darkness and gnashing of teeth. From there he rose up, and, surveying his "dismal situation waste and wild" shouted: "Better to reign in Hell than serve in Heaven" and "here at least we shall be free!" So, characteristically, spoke Milton's Satan.[1]

Pride, which by nature is competitive, leaves us in total isolation. But even from his isolation Satan swims against the currents of life, "wearing himself out in absurd terrifying attempts to reconstruct in the opposite direction the whole world of the Creator."[2] Satan personifies the human pride that ever restlessly strives to re-imagine and reinvent reality and thereby, as his other name Devil (from diabolos, slanderer) suggests, attempts to throw all of life into confusion.

It is not always easy to discern the powers of evil at work even among God's own children. Being the great imitator that he is ("the ape of God" Luther called him) Satan incarnates himself in human beings and human agencies. While these sinister powers cannot finally destroy the true believer (Matt. 24:24), they can do a lot of damage and cause a lot of grief. This holds true especially for those Christians who fail to pay proper attention to these forces. When believers are involved in conflict with one another, when to their surprise their relationships are somehow suddenly being ripped up, when they feel rejected or at least misunderstood, there is every reason to suspect the supernatural agency of the old Deceiver (cf. 1 Tim. 4:1; 2 John 7; Rev. 12:9).

It is not as if we have not been warned. The New Testament is full of admonitions to be wide awake to the operations of him who comes at us with a brilliant smile, like an angel of light, to bring about our undoing (2 Cor. 11:13–15).

It is therefore safer to assume and recognize that Satan exists in the way the Bible says he does and in the way the Christian tradition has confirmed his existence. On all accounts, there is a persistent anti-Christian agent at large, seeking to subvert the work of God the Father, the Son, and the Holy Spirit. While it is a mistake to blame him for all human evil while denying our own complicity in evildoing, it is a major folly to overlook this source. While it may shake the optimism of some individuals about the human condition, at least the recognition of a supernatural agency in the destruction of human life can end the illusion that we can manage the struggle with evil all by ourselves.

I once had a discussion with two leaders of a Christian fellowship. I expressed the conviction that some of the problems I was facing were "of Satan." Aghast at the very suggestion, they looked at me incredulously, and briskly shaking their heads, told me that Satan had absolutely nothing to do with it. This was a surprise to me, for I was talking with individuals who had appointed themselves as leaders of a Christian fellowship. Somehow they flatly ruled out Satan as a major player in the lives of Christian people. They held to the first of two errors cited in this connection by C. S. Lewis (1944) in the Preface to his *Screwtape Letters*: "There are two equal and opposite errors into which our race can fall about the devils. One is to disbelieve in their existence. The other is to believe, and to feel an excessive and unhealthy interest in them. They themselves are equally pleased by both errors." The great Masquerader finds it easier to work with people who do not believe he exists, or who downplay his role in our lives. This is a very serious and costly folly!

The Blindness of Folly

Failure to discern the nature of folly and to stand firm against evil has brought a decline of excellence on all levels of our society. While totalitarianism, in many parts of the world, is on the way out (for the time being), we have no reason whatsoever to be smug. As Americans we are now living in the most violent, corrupt, confused, and immoral period of our history. Probably at no time in American history up until now has there been such widespread immorality and wretchedness.

Why this widespread decline in excellence and explosion of wretchedness? The answer is that so many "good people," so many educated people, so many people in positions of leadership seem to have given up on truth as a transcript of the way things are to be in God's world. In the absence of abiding standards, relativism reigns supreme. With the Bible being ruled out as *the* standard of truth, and with those who hold to it being dismissed as intolerant reactionaries or right wing extremists, our culture is spiraling downward in a whirlpool of subjectivism. The majority of Americans, we are told, do not believe in absolute truth!

The trouble is, as G. K. Chesterton warned years ago, that when people stop believing in God they do not believe in nothing but tend to fall for anything. The road is then clear for calling the absolute relative, and calling the relative absolute; clear for the infantile docility that follows cultish leaders; clear for the self-centered sentiment that drives out the currency of truth; clear for blindly following and supporting immoral leaders; clear for the escapism that renders many individuals incapable of looking reality in the eye; clear for the fanaticism that rides a fragment of truth into absurdity; clear for an unbiblical mysticism that dissolves human life into a cloud of unknowing, and clear for paganism.

As I have repeatedly mentioned in this book, the basic pillars needed for wholesome living are still truth, reason, and faith. All three are essential. Without truth, that is, without a firm grip on fundamental reality, we cannot begin to reason; and without faith we can neither start nor continue our life's journey. Reason is the necessary instrument by which we take a hold of the truth of the gospel and search out the patterns of meaning woven into the fabric of life. Without truth, reason, and faith we inevitably fall for the counterfeit ideas that abound in our culture, and become counterfeit people, the shells of human beings clothed in fluffy pretentiousness—mentally and/or spiritually unhealthy people who are satisfied as long as they live in a "healthy economy." Our folly not only makes us blind, it also leaves us empty. In our emptiness we stuff ourselves compulsively with cotton candy of sweet-tasting nonsense. History is strewn with the wreckage of those who tried to live on it.

The History of Human Folly

Much of history is the record of human folly. In her book *The March of Folly*, Barbara W. Tuckman (1984) defines folly as "the pursuit of policy contrary to self-interest," and describes in detail how "from Troy to Vietnam" the world's leaders have brought devastating events down on their own countries. Imagine: at the very point at which, during World War I, Germany had almost starved Great Britain to death, it ordered its submarine commanders to attack also the ships of neutral countries, thus drawing a largely isolationist United States into the war and tipping the balance of power against itself. Imagine: in 1941, when Japan was the "unstoppable" superpower in the Pacific and sought to rule the countries of the Southeastern Pacific rim as far as Indonesia and even Australia, and could only be stopped by the United States, it dropped bombs on the U.S. Navy at Pearl Harbor and insured U.S. involvement against itself.

Nor is the wisdom which sees these actions as folly only a matter of hindsight. For in both cases there were people who warned the governments in question against the probable outcomes, but were overruled. Ever since the Trojans (against the warnings of its own prophet Laocoon) pulled inside the walls of its city the wooden horse that carried Greek soldiers in its belly, rulers in the Western world have sealed the destruction of their own countries as they "pursued policies contrary to their own interest."

What incredible suffering the world has endured, century after century, because of the willful rejection of God's lifesaving standards of love, wisdom, and knowledge (such as "when your enemy hungers, give him to eat"). Instead, to this very day, some "leaders" will deny food and medicine even to children, and order the bombing of hospitals and marketplaces in "enemy" territory, while terrorists kill worshippers in mosques, synagogues, and churches. Few indeed are the leaders who clearly follow the dictates of God's wisdom and love.

Wars are nearly always counterproductive. The folly of even a single leader, as we have seen, can have incredibly long-lasting and far-reaching effects. Consider the follies of such brutal dictators as Hitler, Stalin, Idi Amin, Ceausescu, and so many others. More than one-half century later many people still reap the unsavory fruits of the wickedness of some of these dictators.

Scripture tells the story of the folly of Rehoboam, the son of King Solomon. When Rehoboam became King of Israel, he did not want to listen to the reasonable demands for mild reform presented to him by most of the tribes of Israel. Unwilling to listen to the solid advice of the wise old men who had previously counseled his father (2 Chron. 10:6), Rehoboam chose to take advice from inexperienced young friends who advised him to treat the people of Israel harshly. Consequently, all but two tribes of Israel revolted under the leadership of the able and well-liked general Jeroboam. Israel was soon divided and has never been united again. The folly of one man lingers on some three thousand years later. Think of it—3000 years later!

Modern world leaders do well to reflect on the folly of Rehoboam. But folly goes much deeper and much further back than King Rehoboam. *Folly has been around on this earth since the days of Adam and Eve.* It was Eve who in the Garden of Eden first believed the Serpent's lie that she would not die if only she ate of the forbidden fruit, and what is more, that she would even become as a "god" (Gen. 3). These lies of Satan are as much alive today as they were then. Today, however, we have far more people who boldly go about proclaiming that they are gods! Those who claim to be gods, however, commit the sin of the anti-christ (2 Thess. 2:4,11). We now have millions of individuals who worship multiple gods, and many others who worship only themselves.

The Recycling of Old Ideas

Many of those who claim personal divinity belong to a loose network of people and organizations that insist we are living in a New Age, and who often follow a set of so-called New Age practices. There is little realistic or reasonable substance to be found in this movement. There is very little good and very much wrong in most of these New Age teachings. Some of their positive contributions, for example in regard to the environment, are greatly overshadowed by their deep involvement in pantheism, occultism, and gnosticism. Though the basic ideas underlying these "isms" are very ancient, they now carry the added meaning of a rejection of Christianity, the dominant religion of the West. And when they are packaged and presented in a series of autobiographies, as in the case of the actress Shirley MacLaine, they may seem appealing and even glamorous.

On this score, Americans are not well prepared to resist an invasion of repackaged pagan errors. In 1994, according to one pollster, 70 percent of all Americans believed there is no absolute truth and a startling 62 percent of "born-again" Christians told the pollster they don't believe in absolute truth either. And five years later, in 1999, we found that polls indicated that most Americans were more concerned with a healthy economy than with having law-abiding, truthful leaders. Half of all Americans believe in ESP; half believe that all religious practices lead to heaven; a quarter believe in reincarnation and "a shockingly large number say they communicate with the dead."[3] We are clearly more than knee-deep into neo-paganism.

The Proliferation of Cults

Cult religions have proliferated over the last few decades, and this is a major concern to all who value choice, liberty, mental health, and freedom of worship and religion. For cults endanger not only the individual, but undermine the entire fabric of family and society. Cult leaders have little interest in freedom of personal choice, the family, or society at large, but, diabolically, often appear in the forefront of so-called family concerns. In actuality, however, these cult leaders seek complete control over their followers. To achieve that goal they will not shrink from employing any means at their disposal, but they especially favor emotional manipulation. Some cult leaders work hard to draw extraordinary amounts of attention to themselves, while others shun all publicity. In some cult publications one repeatedly finds the name and picture of the leader so that it becomes imprinted on the unsuspecting mind of the reader. Cult leaders fondly endow themselves with all manner of pseudo-gifts, powers, abilities, callings, anointings, and especially with their own particular brand of mysticism.

Some cults teach there are no absolutes or moral standards. Others teach salvation by works, causing many of their followers to suffer disproportionately from depression and suicide. Some religious cults teach there is no divine Savior, and others teach that the cult leader is the Savior. Many cults claim that only through their actions (with their blessings) will it be possible to enter the kingdom of heaven or special levels of heaven. Whatever they teach will be based on those special "insights" and other "powers" that are only available through them. *Power, exclusivity, secrecy, control, self-aggrandizement, greed, materialism, emotionalism, and/or deceitful recruitment practices are but some of the characteristics found in cults.*

In some cults there is no forgiveness or hope, and thus no future. Many of the followers in various cults are perpetually enslaved to practices and habits that keep their followers firmly in the clutches of hopelessness. Millions of people spend much of their time, money, and energy, doing—or having others do—mantras, charts, channeling, divinations, readings, and other so-called "spiritual" activities. Many also participate in a good deal of external whitewash and spend lavishly on health parlors and anything that can enhance their image. The cry is for the "good life" which, of course, remains elusive to all who are in bondage to cultism or occultism.

While millions are kept busy working their way into *spiritual ecstasy*, others are hooked on the folly of *nothingness* or, more commonly, the folly of *superconsciousness*. The latter is often used as a kind of transcendental magic, self-transforming science, or even personal divinity. Endless indeed is the parade of fools that pass by, and heartrendingly tragic is the outcome of those who place their trust in untrustworthy leaders, surrendering their very soul into the hands of deception. *Ultimately, of course, it is Satan, the mastermind of evil, who is behind every folly of the past or present.* For then and now, it was and it is Satan who wants us to believe the lie, that we can all be as "gods." Through some cults he teaches that people can be gods now, and through others that this only takes place after death. Having looked at some of Satan's obvious handiwork, let us now consider one of his more subtle activities right in our midst.

Predators in Our Midst

It has always been understood that those who enter into some type of ministerial work have rigorously scrutinized their motives for doing so. It is commonly assumed that these men and women have responded to a special call for ministry. And that their lives, their doctrine, their social and personal conscience, are all in line with the will of God, that these individuals are of good moral character, and that they do not suffer from serious personality disorders or handicapping emotional problems. Furthermore, it is generally assumed that they do not enter into ministerial work for power, control, greed, or worse, for satisfying their roaming sexual fantasies. Most assuredly it is usually taken for granted that those who enter the ministry are genuine believers whose lives are rooted in Christ and who have a close and intimate relationship with Him.

Unhappily, and dangerously so, these assumptions are all too often false! Many are the "wolves in sheep's clothing," who have entered into the "sheep-pen" through some other door. There are many ministers and others who simply lack integrity, humility, or true love. Some of them have grown rich on the backs of the poor. They are strangers to Christ, mere "hirelings." They care not for the sheep. They care only for themselves. Jesus warns us to flee from these individuals. Don't walk, run! It may well be a matter of life or death. There is nothing innocent about a wolf in sheep's clothing. A wolf is a predator and comes to kill and to destroy. Christian overcomers must listen very carefully to the voice of God that comes to us by way of the Scriptures. We must know the way of salvation laid out for us in the Bible and not rest until we have internalized it. We must know the bedrock standards laid down by our heavenly Father and the selfless, self-sacrificing example of our Lord, if we are to be discerning listeners. We must watch for wolves in sheep's clothes, hirelings, thieves and robbers, and flee all those in ministry who are not sanctified in Christ (cf. John 10:1–30).

It is important to be defenders of the faith (Jude), and to stand up for justice, righteousness, and holiness in the church. But this is often a difficult task. Rare, for example, is the wayward minister who confesses his sins, or who does not try to justify unholy and sacrilegious behaviors. And we must not expect too much from church councils either. When it comes to correcting those ministers who have violated their office, church councils may find the whole matter too hot to handle. Comments Plantinga (1995): "People connive everywhere. Family members avert their eyes from domestic abuse that is obvious to outsiders. Church councils connive at humiliation of members by power-hungry pastors who discourage questions and rebuke dissent. These councils show elaborate mercy to their pastor and offer his victims little justice—sometimes listening hospitably to the pastor's explanations, disavowals, and reinterpretations while ostracizing plaintiffs as troublemakers."

Christians can only succeed if they live in harmony with the will of God and are closely walking with the Lord from moment to moment. But the very kindness, compassion, and mercy that we find in Christians can also make them easy targets for abuse. Those who are preying on others nearly always go after lonely, trusting, needy, or otherwise vulnerable individuals. Predators often prey on their helpful assistants, individuals who have come to rely on them, or those who seek their counsel. Predators patiently wait for opportunities, or if necessary, they will skillfully create situations to entrap their victims. They often do so while feigning selfless interest and being ingratiatingly sweet.

Who are these miserable individuals that destroy instead of edify? How prevalent are these predators in the church? We can start looking in the pews. Here we find many individuals who abuse their wives and/or children. Incest in the church is not uncommon.[4] Various forms of sexual and other immorality are quite common. That there is so much immorality among church members comes as no surprise when we consider the great extent of immorality among those who are the leaders of the flock, many of whom are deep into pornography and worse.

The many warnings that God has given us about wolves in sheep's clothing are not to be taken lightly (Matt. 7:15). The watchful overcomer must be especially alert to signs of *manipulation* (skillfully influencing), *intimidation* (instilling some form of fear), and *domination* (persuasively trying to control).[5] The trouble with manipulation, of course, is that the person who is being manipulated is rarely aware of it, otherwise it would not and could not have happened in the first place. How do we resolve these problems? The best way to deal with the problem of folly, within and outside the church, is found in *prevention*. Overcomers must become more realistic and rational in their thinking and behavior. They need to diligently study and take seriously everything that is written in God's Word. The answer, however, is especially to be found in a deeper and deeper walk with our Savior and praying daily for a renewed mind. In conclusion, let us listen to the voice of God in Scripture as it addresses the subject of wolves in sheep's clothing:

> "But these men blaspheme in matters they do not understand. They are like brute beasts, creatures of instinct, born only to be caught and destroyed, and like beasts they too will perish. They will be paid back with harm for the harm they have done. Their idea of pleasure is to carouse in broad daylight. They are blots and blemishes reveling in their pleasure while they feast with you. With eyes full of adultery, they never stop sinning; they seduce the unstable; they are experts in greed—an accursed brood. They have left the straight way. . . ."(2 Pet. 2:12–15).

In my professional work I have met both predators and their victims, and I am sure that the tragedy of wolves in sheep clothes is as acute today, or even more so, as it was then. Nevertheless, let us be thankful for those who have been delivered from this terrible condition. And we certainly need to earnestly pray for others who are still involved in this great evil. All Christian overcomers must rally to the preaching of the gospel, minister to those who walk in darkness, and be true defenders of the faith. In the next chapter we will look at how to resist some common follies.

11

OVERCOMERS RESIST FOLLIES OF ALL KINDS

A famous hymn begins: "My Jesus I love Thee, I know thou art mine; For Thee all the follies of sin I resign. . . ." As I start a new chapter on follies, I painfully realize that we can resign from the obvious follies of sin, but still be far from clear about the less obvious and more intellectual or current fashions of folly. In this chapter I briefly define some of the latter, and end with a call to discernment.

A few common follies, some perennial and some merely fashionable, follow in alphabetical order.

Cultism

Broadly speaking, the term "cult" refers to worship, or the system and rites of a religious belief, and can refer to any religious belief system. But as we use it here, it refers especially to those groups and organizations that follow the teachings of sectarian leaders who hold supreme authority over their followers. These sectarian leaders are usually of the authoritarian charismatic type, and their views often deviate in important respects from the doctrines of historic Christianity. They tend to draw their followers from among the young, elderly, lonely, unsophisticated, and disenfranchised, as well as from among those who have already had cultic experiences. In the United States, as the reader knows, cultism is very popular. Large and small groups of people will more or less blindly follow their favorite teachers, sometimes from place to place across the land. While the major world religions are not viewed as cults, we do find that some subgroups within these organizations may engage in cultic practices. These practices are nearly always marked by *manipulation, intimidation,* and *domination.*

The cult problem, as I discussed in the previous chapter, is a growing one. It is a worldwide problem and it is undoubtedly helpful to have a few definitions about cults. According to one authority a ". . . cult or cultic group (refers) to any one of a large number of groups . . . that forms around a person who claims he or she has a special mission or knowledge, which will be shared with those who turn over most of their decision making to that self-appointed leader. . . . Because cult structure is basically authoritarian, the personality of the leader is all important" (Singer, 1995). An authority on *Christian* cults writes that a cult can be defined as ". . . a group of people gathered about a specific person or person's misinterpretation of the Bible" (Martin, 1985). According to Langone (1993) cults use a variety of techniques, such as sensory bombardment (lengthy lectures and sleep deprivation); breaking ties with family and friends; and hypnotic emotionality (confessional guilt-inducing sessions and stirring songs). All of this is designed to increase a vulnerable person's suggestibility.[1]

Here are ten warning signs of *possible* cult characteristics:

- The leader has little or no accountability.
- The leader demands unquestioning commitment.
- The leader employs hypnotic techniques such as chanting, or prolonged emotionally-charged repetitive music.
- The leader skillfully creates guilt feelings in the followers.
- The leader regularly requests extra financial support.
- The leader keeps the followers from family or former friends.
- The leader fosters socialization only with other followers.

- The leader is elevated above others who are regarded as *not* well-informed, spiritual, or gifted.
- The leader spreads negative or fearful beliefs about "outside" individuals or groups.
- The leader claims special abilities, gifts, or insights that are not available elsewhere.

Even if only a few of these possible warning signs are present, it is worthwhile to have a closer look, to check and double-check. We also might seek two or more opinions from reliable outside sources, and, above all, look closely at the Scriptures for guidance.

Emotionalism

Emotionalism is the habitual practice of placing subjective experiences ahead of objective observations. It often involves the battering of human consciousness into states of altered (more suggestible) consciousness.

Emotionalism is the antithesis of reasonableness and often of truth itself. It is an acquired habit of emotional excitement in response to experiences that are often neither understood nor questioned. It is commonly used to seduce people to agree with something in the marketplace, the home, at work, in politics, or even in the church. Emotionalism has led many people into false doctrine and the enslavement of cultism.

Emotionalism says, "if it feels good, it is good." When used by skillful practitioners, it ensures that unsophisticated victims will seek neither moral nor rational validation. Surely the secret manipulation of human emotions in furthering any cause whatever must be considered evil.

Please note that God does not primarily appeal to our emotions, but to our sensibilities and conscience; not to closed minds but to open minds; not to opinions, fables, presumptions, or hearsay, but to facts. God urges us to seek wisdom, knowledge, and understanding (Prov. 18:15; 1 John 4:1; Gal. 6:7), to test the spirits, and to guard against deception.

God reminds us to search, pray, think, and watch, but emotionalists appeal to the surface emotions and create drama. How translucent this often is in those who feed off their followers' emotions and purses. How adept they are at the use of tears, laughter, and choking cries, and how quickly they can turn these on and off. They may rapidly move from sadness to joy, and from screaming to whispering, always hoping that the right dart will penetrate the right heart at the right moment.

Anyone who *intentionally* invokes emotionalism might do so fraudulently, or because of personal-maladjustment. Dr. Abraham Kuyper, a Dutch theologian, said: "In my opinion, a Christian rather should be averse to the whipped-up emotionality that regales itself on weak nerves and sneaks in sadness from an imaginary world."[2] But we must be more than averse. We must be alert. For whenever a salesperson, politician, teacher, preacher, or anyone else appeals primarily to human emotions rather than to human intellect and volition, then this person is in the business of creating altered states of consciousness—buyer beware!

Fanaticism

Fanaticism is a posture of extremism, or unreasoned enthusiasm, especially in the pursuit of religious causes. While politics has its diary of fanaticism as well ("extremism in the service of one's country is no vice"), religious fanaticism has consistently been the front-runner. Fanatics forget everything else—especially the rules of decency—in the passionate pursuit of a single aim.

Fanatics are blind to everything but their own ideas. They can reduce reality to a single emotional passion. They may trample on all that is fair and human to vent their vindictiveness on those with whom they disagree. And the worst fanatics all too often are the religious fanatics who imagine that God is smiling down on them and opening the gates of paradise for them when they throw a bomb at a school bus, or drive a truck loaded with explosives into a sensitive public building. Religious fanaticism always flourishes when unregenerate or disturbed individuals want to give God a hand.

The Bible offers many examples of religious fanaticism. Remember the story of Shechem, the Canaanite prince who seduced and raped Dinah, Jacob's only daughter (Gen. 34). It was a dastardly act. What the man did next was to ask Jacob for permission to marry his daughter! Now the issue lies before the sons of the covenant. How will they respond? Simeon and Levi treacherously propose that all the men of the town be circumcised (the sign of the covenant!). When they agree and are sore, the sons of the covenant slaughter them and rob them of their wives and children. "Cursed be their anger, so fierce, and their fury, so cruel!," says Jacob on his deathbed (Gen. 49:7), giving a profile of a fanaticism that does not shrink even from treachery with the means of grace to accomplish their ungodly goals. And let's not forget that it was religious fanaticism that infected the mob which cried: "Take him away! Take him away! Crucify him!" (John 19:15; see also Acts 7:57 ff.; Acts 9:1,2).

Fatalism

Fatalism holds that everything in life is predetermined. A fatalist, therefore, is one who believes that we cannot alter our "fixed destiny." Much evidence can be found in the Scriptures that an all-knowing God indeed has everything under control, including our very lives. God, who has a special purpose for everyone, appointed times for everything in our lives. Yet he confronts us with a gospel which calls us to choose to repent from our wicked ways, and offers to give direction to our lives.

There is no fatalism in the message of the Gospel. It is a message of hope. The course and direction of our lives can, by the grace of God, be changed. God, in working out a plan for our lives, invites us to be participators, calling for worship, faith, and obedient living.

Fatalism in the church is bad. But we should also be concerned about the fatalism we find in the secular world. A form of it is belief in astrology, which has repeatedly been proven to be a pseudo-science, a fraud, or worse. Yet millions of people faithfully live by the constellations and conjunctions of stars as reported in their daily newspapers. Astrology is one of the great and persistent follies that brings in millions of dollars each year to those who make it their business, but also leads millions of people astray.

Fatalism is also implicit in the belief that karma, or "the law of justice," determines our entire life. According to this belief, if we are good, we will be reincarnated into a better life. Conversely, if we live a bad life we will be reincarnated into a worse life. Many people believe that they must go through various bodily existences until they are finally assimilated into the "Absolute." Happily, the Bible teaches a more hopeful message: there is but one death and one resurrection (Heb. 9:27). Fatalism is escapist folly.

Hedonism

The subtitle of John Piper's book, *Desiring God* (1986) is "Meditations of a Christian Hedonist." If we find that combination "Christian hedonist" jarring, let us think again. The desire for happiness is universal: all human beings, including those who kill themselves, desire happiness. The end of man, says the old Catechism, is to glorify God and to enjoy him forever." One end, not two. So we glorify God by enjoying Him and all He gives us forever. The problem, says C. S. Lewis, is not that our desire for happiness is too strong but too weak. We are like ignorant children who go on making mud pies in a slum because they cannot imagine what is meant by the offer of a holiday at the sea (see C. S. Lewis, *The Weight of Glory and Other Addresses*, 1965, 2).

Oh, but hedonism is about the pursuit of pleasure, we say. Well, is God opposed to pleasure? In his right hand, says the psalmist (16:11), are pleasures forevermore. But are we not to deny ourselves? Yes, but only as a means, not an end. That end is to follow Jesus ". . . who for the joy that was set before him endured the cross. . . ." (Heb. 12:2).

Then why do I treat hedonism in a list of human follies? Answer: because, in its pagan or neopagan forms, it refers to the dogma that pleasure, even self-indulgent sensual pleasure, is the principal good in human life. It concerns the inordinate pursuit of pleasure in eating, drinking, gaming, sex, and so forth, in total disregard of God's wise directives and boundaries. And when we look at the results—drunkenness, family breakups, health problems, car accidents, sexually transmitted diseases, poverty, and crime—we know that in following a neopagan hedonistic lifestyle people are passionately sawing off the branch they are sitting on. For a more in-depth discussion on Christian happiness, see *The Renewed Mind* (Brandt, 1999).

Humanism

Historically, the term "humanism" is associated with the revival of human learning in the second half of the fifteenth century in Europe. This revival of human learning included not only the fine arts and classic literature but also the natural sciences and human ethics. It was humane in that it featured human values and emotions as these are manifested in the arts and in human society as a whole.

In its more modern usage humanism has its roots in the "Enlightenment of the Eighteenth Century." In this usage human beings are not *a* source of value but *the only* source. It insists that individuals are emancipated from every authority, human or divine, and to be guided only by their own theoretical and practical reason. Contemporary humanism is thoroughly secular. According to this view the world is not created but simply exists. Humankind is part of nature. The human species arises from the animal world and does not bear the image of God. Science provides the only avenue to knowledge of the universe. The end of humankind lies in some form of self-realization, not in knowing and serving God.

The Christian faith, based as it is on mankind's creation in the image of God and Christ as the Son of God incarnate in human flesh, is opposed to all that dehumanizes or debases human beings. It regards the realization of true humanity, not as the product of human self-effort, but as the result of the work and the Spirit of Jesus Christ (see *Encyclopedia of Biblical and Christian Ethics*, 1987, pp. 189–190).

Narcissism

Narcissism, in the popular sense, is the excessive love of one-self. Psychologists distinguish primary narcissism from secondary narcissism. Primary narcissism is normal in the early stages of child-hood when a child is concerned mainly to gratify its own bodily functions. Secondary narcissism is a settled neurotic trait occur-ring in later life as a result of withdrawing one's energies from oth-ers and becoming self-absorbed (Sutherland, 1989). Beyond this we can speak of narcissistic lifestyles centered in self-gratification by any means whatever (Lasch, 1979).

Luther describes the general phenomenon of narcissism when he analyzes the nature of sin. "Due to original sin our nature is so curved in upon itself at its deepest levels that . . . it does not even know that in this wicked, twisted, crooked way, it seeks every-thing, including God, only for itself' (Luther, 1961).[3] An excel-lent description of narcissism is by Lewis B. Smedes (1990):

> Narcissistic people do not see other people, or feel other people; they only see and feel themselves in the mirror of other people. Another person *exists* only when she exists for the narcissist.
>
> Narcissists require everyone close to them to function as a reflection in which they, the narcissists, can see themselves as lovable. Friends exist only to fill the gaping hole in their empty egos. As long as their friends approve, they feel worthy. If they find a fault, they become enemies. When loved ones fog the mirror in which narcissists must see their own worth, the loved ones are betrayers. In this way narcissists hold everyone else hostage to their own aching needs.

But what lies behind this narcissistic preoccupation with self? Traditionally the attempt to understand it has focused on pride or self-idolatry. And pride, by nature competitive, isolates itself from others. But the truth may be somewhat more complex. In the an-cient myth of Narcissus, the coldhearted 16-year-old with the face of a Greek god rejected all who followed him. One of his rejected suitors, feeling vindictive, prayed that Narcissus himself might fall in love and be rejected. That prayer was heard by Nemesis who led him to a pool of water to drink. It was there that Narcissus saw and fell in love with his own reflection. He was self-hypnotized and unable to look away. In reaching out to his reflection he found it reached out to him and in withdrawing from it, it withdrew from him. At last, in despair, he described his tragedy by saying: "My loved one's mine: possession makes me poor" (Ovid, *Metamorphoses*, Book III, E. E. Watts translation, 63). Possession makes Narcissus poor because what he loves is a phantom. Selfencapsulation, outwardly the action of self-idolatry, is "essentially a defensive maneuver in the face of an overwhelming sense of worthlessness" (Sugarman, 1976).

This is what I have said elsewhere about the so-called narcissistic personality:

> Individuals with narcissistic personality styles like to fantasize about the great things they will attain. With an unhealthy need to impress (themselves, as well as others) they crave attention and admiration. Narcissistic persons are eager to talk about the "wonderful" things they have done, or are going to do; the many places they have been to, the many people they have "served," and the important people they know, or have been associated with. When criticized, they will respond with indifference or rage. They feel so superior that they claim entitlement to special treatment. Skilled at manipulation, intimidation, and domination, they often exploit others (Brandt, 1998).

The narcissistic search for one's self can, in essence, be viewed as a flight from the connected self that God created. In the absence of a connected self, and through preoccupation with a phantom self, despair is inevitable, however we dress it up. "What a wretched man that I am! Who will rescue me from this body of death? Thanks be to God—through Jesus Christ our Lord!" (Rom. 7:24, 25).

Occultism

The word occultism (occult, hidden, secret) points to secret influences that cannot be grasped with the mind. In the strict sense it refers to secret practices known only to initiates. In Western occultism we encounter such practices as astrology, channeling, crystal ball gazing, divination, palmistry, Satanism, spiritualism, the Ouija ("yes"- "yes" in French and German respectively) Board, and witchcraft.

In our day, a time in which numerous Christians have only the skimpiest knowledge of the teaching of Scripture, some forms of the occult again attract many unwary seekers of spiritual experience. Especially the occultism (reincarnation and channeling) of the New Age Movement has many followers.[4]

To such "seekers of spiritual experience" it needs to be said that these occult experiences are off limits to Christian believers. They lead us away from our Lord Jesus Christ into a domain of secrecy and darkness, as the word *occultism* itself suggests. God is dead-set against it. "Let no one be found among you who . . . practices divination or sorcery, interprets omens, engages in witchcraft, or casts spells, or who is a medium or spiritist or who consults the dead" (Deut. 18:10–11). "When men tell you to consult mediums and spiritists, who whisper and mutter, should not a people inquire of their God? Why consult the dead on behalf of the living? To the law and to the testimony! If they do not speak according to this word, they have no light of dawn" (Isa. 8:19–20).

One thing is abundantly clear; Christian overcomers must be alert to the powers of darkness, regardless of whatever "benign" or "beautiful" form in which it may present itself. There is nothing right and everything wrong with occultism. Sadly, even many Christians have fallen victim to the evil of occultism. Writes Dr. Hobart E. Freeman (1969):

> There has never been a time in history when the warnings against the dangers of occultism (all forms of fortune-telling; magic, spiritism, false religious cults) were more needful than the present time in which we live (p. 3). . . . Countless (people) have been subjected to the influences and deceptions of spiritualism, assuming everything supernatural is of God, and mistaking the powers of darkness for the power of God (p. 4) . . . psychics, who claim their "gift" is from God, are deluding multitudes, including many professing Christians, ministers, and

religious leaders, who naively accept everything supernatural as divine, oblivious to the fact that Satan can also perform great signs and wonders (2 Th. 2:9f.).

It goes beyond the scope of this book to write in too much detail on the incredible influence of the powers of darkness in the lives of all too many ill informed, naive, or otherwise vulnerable individuals. But I would like to point out that overcomers *must* be alert to the follies that surround them, and *must* learn to stand up against them! And that can only be done with the power of the Holy Spirit:

> Finally, be strong in the Lord and in his mighty power. Put on the full armor of God so that you can take your stand against the devil's schemes. For our struggle is not against flesh and blood, but against the rulers, against the authorities, against the powers of this dark world and against the spiritual forces of evil in the heavenly realms. Therefore put on the full armor of God, so that when the day of evil comes, you may be able to stand your ground, and after you have done everything, to stand. Stand firm then, with the belt of truth buckled around your waist, with the breastplate of righteousness in place, and with your feet fitted with the readiness that comes from the gospel of peace. In addition to all this, take up the shield of faith, with which you can extinguish all the flaming arrows of the evil one. Take the helmet of salvation and the sword of the Spirit, which is the word of God. And pray in the Spirit on all occasions with all kinds of prayers and requests. With this in mind, be alert and always keep on praying for all the saints (Eph. 6:10–18).

Corrie ten Boom, who has been mentioned several times in this book, was a great overcomer. She lived by the love, voice, mind, spirit, and will of God. She had a winning attitude, and a healthy personality. She lived by truth, reason, and faith. She was a wonderful apostle of love. She radiated kindness, mercy, and forgiveness. But, Corrie ten Boom also had discernment, and she was a great defender of the faith. She understood the powers of evil and she always stood up against them.

Corrie ten Boom was sad that so many individuals, Christians included, failed to recognize the insidious nature of evil that so often *comes under the disguise of good,* ". . . travelling over the world; and having met so many people—even dear servants of the Lord—who, though surrounded by the powers of darkness, the devil and the demons, do not recognize them, and do not know how to deal with them . . . (Ten Boom, 1963)."

Understanding the powers of evil, and dealing with them, is an absolute necessity if we are to be overcomers in this world. Here is Corrie ten Boom's succinct summary of the powers of darkness:

The devil or Satan is introduced to us as a person who opposes God and His work (see Gen. 3:1; Rom. 15:22). He is the "god of this world," who blinds the minds of the people to the truths of God's Word (2 Cor. 4:4; Eph. 2:2). Having rebelled against God, he was cast out of heaven; then he caused man's fall in paradise. Jesus calls him the father of lies, a liar, a murderer (John 8:44). He works often as an "angel of light" (2 Cor. 11:14), seeking the ruin of the elect! (1 Pet. 5:8). But he was cursed of God. Jesus triumphed over him at the Cross of Calvary (1 John 3:8) and in His resurrection, and he will finally be condemned and destroyed (Rev. 20). There are many kinds of demons, and they afflict people in various ways (see Matt. 12:22; 17:15–18; Luke 13:16). Also, they bring false doctrine (1 Tim. 4:1–4), trying to seduce the elect (Matt. 24:24), oppressing (Acts 10:38), obsessing, and possessing people. They know Jesus, and recognize His power and tremble (Matt. 8:29). For them, hell is the final destination, as it is for Satan (ten Boom, 1963).

The Importance of Discernment

John Cassian, a fourth-century monk, tells us in one of his books about an all-night conference between the blessed Antony and a group of monks who sought out his wisdom. The talk was about perfection. Together they conducted a searching inquiry into which virtue and which discipline would keep a monk from falling a prey to the deceptions of the devil and lead him to the summit of perfection. Some said fasting was the secret of attaining union with God; others stressed detachment from the things of the world; still others opted for the works of hospitality, as that which had the greatest promise.

Finally, after most of the night had been spent, the blessed Antony spoke up, saying something like this: "All the things you have mentioned are necessary and helpful. Still, I have seen many men come to disaster who followed these surefire roads to perfection. Not only did they not finish their course, but they fell into deep delusion. What was wrong? The virtuous activities of which you were talking all flourished among them. What was lacking was one thing and one thing only: discernment. No other cause can be found for their downfall."[5]

Just how timely are the words of the blessed Antony?—Very! Discernment not only keeps us from veering too far to the right in an excess of zeal, and from steering too far to the left into an attitude of carelessness. It is also essential if we are to live by truth and reason. Discernment is the opposite of folly.

Of course, it is good to remind ourselves that we must not "expect certainty where it cannot exist."[6] Our discernment is never 100 percent perfect. For that reason we need to share what we are seeing with others who are looking at the same situation with us. These others do not have perfect vision either, of course, and they could also be wrong. But it is also possible that they could point out to us things we had missed. Discernment grows best in a community of discernment. That is not a community in which everyone listens to a single guru, but one in which each one listens—truly listens—to everyone else. In a community of shared discernment we do not shout at each other, but listen to each other because we genuinely believe that others may see reality a little more accurately than we do. Let us have a look at two types of discernment: mental and spiritual discernment.

Mental Discernment

In order to have mental (cognitive/intellectual) discernment, we must again call to mind the three questions for *sound decision making*, which we discussed earlier: *Is it realistic? Is it rational? Is it positive?* Applying these criteria to certain questionable ideas we are able to list a number of characteristics under separate headings as follows:

Folly	*Discernment*
Truth is subjective, and purely personal.	Truth is objective, and universal.
Altered states of consciousness provide enlightenment.	A healthy, normal state of consciousness is essential to realism, reason, and faith.
There are no moral absolutes.	Moral absolutes are non-negotiable, universal, and essential to our survival as a race.
Human beings are divine.	With the exception of Jesus Christ, the uniquely beloved Son of God, human beings are fallen, fallible, imperfect, and sinful, but redeemable by the grace of God.
Good and evil are two sides of the same coin.	Good and evil are diametrically opposed to each other.
Human beings can perfect themselves here on earth.	Human beings are not only limited by their humanness, but are by nature in bondage to sin. Only God can save and perfect them.
Human beings can live perfectly well within the horizons of a material world.	Human beings need to look beyond the horizons of a material world.
Human beings are fully able to manage the issues of life and death on their own.	Human beings only know in part and were never intended to manage life and death apart from divine revelation.
Selfishness is normal, natural, and justifiable.	Selfishness in the lives of human beings created for community is death.

Folly	Discernment
If something looks good, feels good, and sounds good, it is good.	Things are only good if they meet divine standards of goodness.
Hiddenness and secrecy are to be treasured.	Hiddenness and secrecy are suspect in God's world, for God values openness and universal truth.
A person's fate is unalterable	God invites us to choose between blessings and curses as genuine options.
The cause of world peace and prosperity requires a one-world government.	One-world government, which could only be enforced by a dictatorship, would be the death of freedom and conscience.
Human beings can, if they wish, become gods or goddesses and populate their own planets.	It is science fiction to believe that human beings can become gods and goddesses.
It is good to pursue pleasure at all cost.	It is spiritual, mental, emotional, physical, and social death, to pursue pleasure as the ultimate good.
Humankind is at the center of the universe.	The idea that humankind is at the center of the universe is dysfunctional because untrue.
Everything is essentially the same.	The idea that essentially all things are the same is a denial of the diversity of things.
Non-Christian dogma is compatible with a Christian worldview.	A Christian worldview can flourish only on the basis of Christian dogma.

Spiritual Discernment

There is no other school of spiritual discernment that compares with the Bible. The Bible is a singularly focused book: it is thematically built around the coming kingdom of one God. It is also singularly rich in its diversity: it contains historical books, prophetic books, wisdom books, gospels, letters, and apocalyptic books. It reflects the entire range of human experience and thought. But through it all there comes to us a single voice, the voice of the Father, the Son, and the Holy Spirit. Those who have the Spirit of Christ in them will pick up the special sound of that voice speaking to them in Scripture. It is by that voice that Jesus' followers will test all other claimants to their attention or loyalty.

Today we live in a pluralist world: the world of many religions and cults. Pluralism, however, does not mean that we can accept all religions and moral commitments as equally valid. The very fact of pluralism requires of us that we sharpen and enrich our powers of spiritual discernment.

Discerning Spiritual Truth

Some of the more obviously false religions and cults can be quickly checked against the Bible, which teaches that there is only:

- *One God*: Deut. 4:35; Isa. 43:10; 44:8; 45:5; 1 Tim. 2:5; 1 Cor. 8:5–7; Eph. 4:4–6.
- *One Christ*: Isa. 7:14; John 1:14, 18; John 3:16; Rom. 1:4; 1 Cor. 15:17.
- *One Holy Spirit*: John 15:26; 16:13.
- *One Kind of Human Being*: Rom. 3:10, 23; 1 John 1:8–10.
- *One Redeemer*: Eph. 1:7; 1 Pet. 1:18–19; Heb. 9:22; 10:12, 14; Rev. 1:5–6.
- *One Salvation*: John 3:6, 18, 36; Rom. 3:24; 5:7–8; 10:4; Eph. 2:8–9; Acts 4:12.
- *One Death*: Heb. 9:27.
- *One Final Judgment*: Rev. 20:12.
- *One Moral Standard*: Rom. 13:8; Gal. 6:2; Col. 3:14; Eph. 5:1, 2; Jas. 2:8.
- *One Aspiration*: Phil. 3:13–15.

Many of the false religions and cults deny the divinity of Christ, or that Jesus is the one and only Redeemer and Savior. Others deny salvation by grace through faith, again others teach reincarnation (a succession of lives and death), deny the validity of biblical standards, or teach that there is no enduring moral standard (all is relative). It takes only a few moments daily to read the scriptures and to discern these false, and even outright heretical, teachings.

To show that some false religions and cults do not even come close to Bible truth is one thing. It is another thing to understand the broader aspects of the spirit world. Whether people like it or not, we are living in more than a merely material, organic, or physical world. The truth is that we are living in a spirit world (Neh. 9:6; Ps. 148:2–5; Col. 1:16).

Even our everyday language bears witness to this. We may say that someone is in good spirits or in bad spirits. Many times we pay little attention to these statements and interpret them to mean that a person is either in a good or bad mood. However, the truth goes much deeper. Our language reflects that human beings are also spiritual beings and can be influenced by either God's healing spirit of love, or Satan's destroying spirit of hate.

Most human beings have an opportunity, and thus responsibility, to choose what they wish to do with their mental, emotional, and spiritual lives. Those who know the gospel are free to make the momentous choice between serving the Lord and serving the old self—between serving God or idols.

It is a false and dangerous teaching that good or evil is relative and exists only in our minds. The evidence is overwhelming that good and evil does exist outside of our minds, and can enter our minds if we allow this to happen. To deny the power of good or evil is simply to deny the facts of life.

Discerning Spiritual Error

Spiritual oppression or possession does exist. The Bible warns us against: *seducing spirits* (1 Tim. 4:1); *occultism and sorcery* (Exod. 20:3–5; Gal. 5:19– 21; Rev. 21:8); *evil spirits* (Deut. 18:9–12); *and "asking counsel of one that has a familiar spirit"* (1 Chron. 10:13, 14), that is, of a *medium*. Participating in any of these events is a serious transgression in the eyes of God. To more fully understand God's view of the occult world it is helpful to read the following passages in the Bible: Deut. 18:9–14; Exod. 7:11–12; 22:18; Lev. 19:26, 31; 20:6, 27; 1 Chron. 10:13–14; 2 Kings 21:5–6; Isa. 2:6; 8:19; Jer. 27:9–10; Acts 8:9–11; 16:16–18; Gal. 5:19–21; Rev. 21:8; 22:15.

At first it may appear that we must be scholars or theologians in order to discern doctrinal error. Happily, this is not true. The average person is quite capable of detecting those teachings that go directly against the Word of God. For example, if the Bible repeatedly states that there is only one God, any teaching to the contrary is heresy. Yet, we encounter individuals who contend that they are "gods," or that they are "little gods." We do not need special training to know that any claim, by anyone, that he or she is a god, goes directly against the teachings of Scripture (cf. Gen. 3; Deut. 4:35; Isa. 43:10; 44:8; 45:5; 1 Tim. 2:5; and 1 Cor. 8:5–7). What is required of us is to read the Bible ourselves, or in study groups, and to think truthfully and rationally.

There are many reasons why false teachers, preachers, and prophets make so many conquests. Firstly, we often have short memories, we pay little attention to what is being said, quickly forget what we hear, and don't even check to see whether or not prophecies come true. We jump to conclusions before the evidence is in. Secondly, we readily accept false teachings because many teachers and preachers claim a *special status* with God—a status we dare not question.

What are some telltale external characteristics of false teachers and prophets? We know that they often are arrogant, self-righteous, self-proclaimed, self-appointed, haughty, unrepentant, self-centered, secretive, and mystical. They have little to no interest in hard work or the poor but they do have an overriding interest in fame, power, influence, wealth, and direct control over others. They love to manipulate, intimidate, and dominate.

The Bible tells us that false teachers *mock the ways of old* (Jer. 6:16); *are greedy* (2 Pet. 2:3; Acts 8:20); *insist on being mediators between God and man* (1 Tim. 2:5); *think they are above criticism* (Acts

17:11; Col. 2:18–19; 2 Tim. 3:16–17); *make prophecies that fail to come true* (Deut. 18:22; Jer. 23:25–26; 24–26); or, *only prophesy positive events* (Isa. 30:10–11; Jer. 6:14; 23:16; 2 Tim. 4:2–4; Col. 2:8).

The burden is on every believer to test prophets, teachers, preachers, spirits, doctrines, revelations, and so forth. This burden would not have been placed on ordinary people by God (1 Cor. 14:29; 1 Jhn 4:1) if they were not capable of doing so. God holds us responsible precisely because we can be held responsible. If we can observe, think, and test, then we must do so. Jesus Himself tells us: "Many will say to me on that day, 'Lord, Lord, did we not prophesy in your name, and in your name drive out demons and perform many miracles?' Then I will tell them plainly 'I never knew you. Away from me you evildoers!'" (Matt. 7:22–23).

Discerning All Things With Love

Finally, there is no greater need and no greater reward than to discern the love and power of God. It is God who is ultimately victorious over every evil thing. To discern the love and power of God requires that we personally know who God is. The Bible tells us that God is love and that God is a spirit. Further, that if we do not have the spirit of love, we cannot possibly know God (1 John 3:14).[7] Rather we shall be found helpless, powerless, empty-headed, and destined for abject misery and total failure.

Even as we consider the many faces of folly in the world and all the evil power of Satan behind most of these instances of folly, we need to acknowledge that God has fundamentally overcome all this. While spiritual gifts are wonderful, and knowledge and wisdom are important, it is ultimately only God who is truly in control. The objective reality that God lives in our hearts, that He does exist independently of our faith, that He is indeed the Alpha and Omega, the great I AM, and that indeed "nothing is impossible with Him" brings victory to every overcomer in Christ (1 John 5:4,5).

As we observe evil powers and principalities, and the unfolding of this Age of Folly, we need to remember that only love can and will conquer evil. We must love those who are in bondage or trouble. Whatever they believe, however steeped in error, we still must reach out in love, for we are not warring against flesh and blood, but against deception, evil, spiritual blindness, and sin.

If we are indeed overcomers in this Age of Folly, it is only because of Christ, for it is He who is Victor; it is He who paid the price. Because He is Victor we, too, can be victorious. But even the selfless love of God is of no use to us unless we avail ourselves of it. We must accept God's love and let God's love work in our lives, for all is in vain unless we have God's love (cf.1 Cor. 13:1–7).

Whatever challenge we face in this Age of Folly, we are not helpless. We have everything we need to be overcomers: the truth of the Gospel, the power of reason, and Jesus Christ our "blessed hope" (Titus 2:13). For the Son of God is alive and well, the Holy Spirit is alive and well, and God is alive and well. He is fully in control. The love of God is as infinite as God Himself and He reminds us that indeed nothing can separate us from His love (Rom. 8:38–39). It is an all-powerful love that heals, saves, restores, brings peace, wholeness, joy, happiness, and every other blessing.

We must remember that all of us are imperfect, fallible, and sinful, and that we all come "short of God's glory and righteousness." *It is especially important to understand that whatever has been said in this chapter is not to be construed as an attack on people or as a judgment of them. Our focus here is not on the individuals who perpetrate follies, but rather on their beliefs and practices.*

I am all too aware that human beings are always at various stages of development, be it in the physical, mental, or spiritual realm. We mature at different speeds. Likewise it is possible to be more mature in one area and less mature in another. We may find individuals who have a lot of faith but lack common sense, or vice versa. There are many kind and sincere individuals who are involved with dangerous cultic practices or other follies. But sincere or insincere, the battle is not with these individuals. Our one and only battle is with evil, the follies of sin: ". . . our struggle is . . . against the powers of this dark world and against the spiritual forces of evil in the heavenly realms" (Eph. 6:12).

We are clearly living in an Age of Folly, where the battle is on for people's minds and ultimately their eternal souls. It is important to take time out to stop and think, to reflect on our life, to consider our lifestyle, to evaluate our beliefs. Are we foolish or wise? *Are we overcomers?*

Part Five:

The Perseverance
of Overcomers

12

OVERCOMERS PRESS ON TOWARD EXCELLENCE

In their life here on earth many individuals become overwhelmed by the many difficulties they continually face. "Life," we concluded earlier, "*is* difficult." Regrettably, all too many persons succumb to difficulties—they are overcome by them. Overcomers, on the other hand, continue to persevere until they reach their goal. Christian and non-Christian overcomers have many similar traits. Both, for example, have winning attitudes, and both, hopefully, have healthy personality styles. Christian overcomers, however, also have additional traits—essential Christian ones. Among other things, we find that they have yielded their own imperfect will to the perfect will of God, bringing them victory over sin, death and the grave. The final chapter in this book highlights the importance of being *an overcomer in Christ*.

To be or not to be," wrote Shakespeare "that is the question." How to succeed rather than fail. How to have excellence rather than wretchedness. These are pressing questions in our modern society. Are we going to overcome evil, or are we going to be overcome by it? Most of us are aware of at least some of the horrendous problems that plague our society, and indeed our entire world—a world filled with all manner of evil. Things have to change. Meaning has to be brought back into the lives of multitudes of lost adolescents and adults. But there can be no meaning without values, and no values without some absolute standards of civilized and moral conduct.

Sometime ago I shared with the editor of a British psychotherapy journal that there is a great demand in the United States for Christian counselors and therapists, a demand that seems to outweigh the demand for non-Christian therapists. Why? Because nearly all secular programs over the past decades have failed to deliver! Millions upon million of dollars have been spent and are being spent in an attempt to make people happier, but there is no power on earth that can achieve these goals.

This is what I have said earlier:

In spite of many governmental, educational, and private programs, and the spending of billions of dollars on "medications," the emotional health of this nation continues to decline. In the meantime, millions of unhappy and often desperate individuals are frantically searching for a modicum of happiness in their lives.

Lacking insight into the nature of their predicament, unable to deal with the many stressors around them, and often devoid of a moral or spiritual anchor, millions of individuals are on a futile search. Futile, because a lasting solution to unhappiness can only be found in a fundamental and permanent change in our mental, emotional, and spiritual orientation.

We must rid ourselves of the misconception that we are merely helpless bystanders on the road to happiness, wellness, and success. We must rid ourselves of the notion that heredity and environment control our destiny—that we are mere pawns being moved across the chessboard of life by powerful external forces. While other individuals and many of life's events may provide various circumstances over which we can make ourselves happy or unhappy, the fact remains that most of us, at least in our society, have the final say over our emotional wellness (Brandt, 1999).

It is a fact of life that no fallible human being or organization is going to deliver us from the destructive influences of an evil world—

a sickness and crime-ridden world that is bent on destroying everything that is good and noble, beautiful, and worthwhile.

Darkness is not interested in light. It wants to extinguish every ray of hope that flows from even the smallest candle. Whether in the hands of single individuals or in the hands of organized groups, evil lurks everywhere. I believe that at no time in human history has there been a greater all-out attack by the forces of evil to destroy our very civilization.

The good news, however, is that light is stronger than darkness, and just as Communism, Fascism, Nazism, and other forms of evil were overcome by that light of truth, so shall we see paganism, terrorism and other scourges of mankind wither away. Just as the walls of Jericho (Joshua 5) came tumbling down, and the Berlin wall came down in our generation (which few believed to be possible), so shall the walls of evil undertakings crumble under the hand of God. How wonderful that light and love are victorious.

In the meantime, however, overcomers must be alert to the many evils that are the "order" of the day. In addition to the countless readily observable and steadily growing destructive forces in our society,[1] there are also many covert and subtle movements at work which try to destroy the very fabric of our Christian civilization, for example, the cultic and occultic practices that have been discussed in previous chapters.

It is impossible to be an overcomer in this deceitful world without *truth, reason,* and *faith.* In this book I have only barely touched on the dangers that are lurking in the places that people least expect. I would have preferred to not mention negative things in this book, but then it would have been one of those misleading books that are so prevalent nowadays: false books, like false prophets, that lull people to sleep, or talk only about good things. *No power of positive thinking, for example, can make us into overcomers unless we first have our feet on a solid foundation of truth and reason.*

Remember, it is not a luxury to be an overcomer in this world—it is a necessity. For either we overcome hardships, limitations, injustices, and unfairness or we are overcome by them. Either we work hard, and strive for excellence, or we shirk our responsibility and be overcome by wretchedness. It is not possible to be a neutral observer or bystander. It is not possible to be uninvolved. We are either "in" or "out."

The forces of evil overpower the powerless—the naive, the ill-informed, or the otherwise vulnerable. Here we may find those who seek peace at all cost and are afraid to assert themselves; those who cannot distinguish between "charming" predators and friendly individuals; those who lack knowledge and wisdom, and who cannot discern between folly and reason; those who believe the evil lie that we must trust our feelings and do whatever feels good; and those who have been deeply hurt and are desperate for nurturance—love-hungry, needy individuals who readily fall into the traps of the many wolves in sheep's clothing. Others who may be overpowered include those who somehow believe that a person can be successful without hard work, well-informed without studying, healthy without a decent diet, financially secure without saving, or a Christian without self-denial.

The road of life is built on a hill with a steep incline. There is no standing still without falling helplessly backward into the coils of wretchedness. Those who think they can be idle bystanders in the battle for the mind soon find themselves mindless—deprived of realistic discernment, rational choice, and positive action. The battle between good and evil is not so much fought around us, as within us. Every human mind is a battlefield where a life and death struggle is taking place between the forces of light and darkness. To live in a world so starkly divided between the forces of good and evil is difficult enough for those who have no clear vision about themselves or the world at large, but it is especially difficult for those who have no vision of God's redemptive power, or who refuse to listen to Him: "Where there is no revelation, the people cast off restraint; but blessed is he who keeps the law" (Prov. 29:18).

It is also virtually impossible to succeed as an overcomer in isolation. God teaches us to help one another in our quest for happiness and wellness. He wants us to live in communities of faith, to worship with fellow believers, and to support and sustain one another. A community with God is blessed with the power of God, but a community without God is powerless.[2] In a godless community, we find those who have no inheritance to share other than selfish competition at best, and murderous hatred at worst.

The Godless Community of the Alienated

The Godless community is a sad place to behold. It is a community of alienated persons who are like rudderless ships on stormy and treacherous seas. It is a place void of binding ethics, wholesome values, or positive standards. It is a community of relativism and opportunism, a place where the only acceptable absolute is that there is "absolutely no God." The only way to really fit in with such a community is to deny the existence of objective reality, to refute logic, and doubt everything.[3]

The Godless community is an atheistic, irreligious, selfish and impious community. A place where manipulation, intimidation, and domination are the order of the day. A place where emotional, physical, and sexual abuse are normal fare. A place where adultery, deceit, pornography, and sexual perversions are quite acceptable. It is here that sociopathic and narcissistic deceivers are adored, defended, and followed. It is here that those who live moral lives will be laughed at. It is here that those who are appointed to uphold the laws of the land will be villified. Those who uphold God's moral will are scorned here for their ethical standards, values, or self-denial. In a Godless community people of honor are seen as abnormal. They are misfits in a community where wrong is called right, and right is called wrong. Even Christians, who live or work in these kinds of surroundings, are sometimes influenced by them.

The good news is that we can escape from Godless communities. God has already prepared the way. "In this world," Jesus reminds us, "you will have trouble. But take heart! I have overcome the world" (John 16:33). God challenges us to not be overcome by evil, but, to overcome evil with good (Rom. 12:2 1). "Who is it that overcomes the world?" writes John the Apostle, "Only he who believes that Jesus is the Son of God" (1 John 5:5). And it is this same Jesus who calls us out to be overcomers with Him: "To him who overcomes I will give the right to eat of the tree of life, which is in the paradise of God" (Rev. 2:7). There were many trees in paradise, but only one was in the midst, the "tree of life" which was lost to us in the fall. But Jesus Christ, our Savior and Redeemer, has restored the tree of life, even as He has restored our lives.[4]

The choice to either overcome evil or to be overcome by it is one that all of us will continue to face until our spirit departs from our body. Salvation brings us the ultimate victory over the grave and death, it does not, however, relieve us from a lifelong task—a task of diligently working for a transformed, victorious, and abundant life. All of our life we must be ready and willing to press on toward excellence in Christ. To help us in this task we do well to seek a committed community of joint-heirs in Christ. Let us now consider such a community.

The God-filled Community of Joint Heirs

One wonderful aspect of the kingdom community is that it is made up of joint heirs with Christ (Rom. 8:17), fellow heirs with former non-Christians (Eph. 3:6), and fellow heirs with the descendants of Abraham (Gal. 3:29). In this community, no one works just for a living—all work for a greater goal. All work primarily out of love—for God, and for others. In this community there is no superior or inferior social status: all its members are brothers and sisters, friends and disciples of Christ. Joint heirs with Him of an unfading inheritance of goodness, greatness, and glory. Together they constitute a community of the children of God—imagine!— who were cherished by God before they knew Him. It is a community defined by faith, hope, and love, and can therefore (actually as well as potentially) be a place of overflowing joy.

In such a community its members are greatly blessed by sharing the Word of God, the love of God, the communion table, the fellowship of believers, praise and worship, and many other blessings. It is clear that overcomers need to be members of a vital fellowship of faith—a place where the leadership is fully committed to sound gospel preaching and worship, the ministry of reconciliation, sound educational programs for adults and children alike, and an active membership involvement in mutual care and community outreach. The kingdom community fosters growth in spiritual fitness, as long as it is grounded in one of the great evangelical traditions. It is rather difficult for many, if not most, community members to fully appreciate, or understand, the Word of God apart from the kingdom community. For the Word of God is a living word that needs to be discussed, studied, shared, and applied in the daily lives of the community members.[5]

All of this is not surprising, for the Bible is a book that took shape in the community of faith. Not only the letters of the apostle Paul, but also the Song of Solomon, was written specifically for the community of faith—the kingdom community! The Apostle calls this community of faith the body of Christ. There is no question at all that overcomers need to be nurtured in the context of a truly Christian body. To have a renewed mind is to have the mind of Christ. But this mind does not go it alone: it is a mind that defers to others, exalts and blesses others. The renewed mind is the mind of selfless servanthood: "Do nothing out of selfish ambition or vain conceit, but in humility consider others better than yourselves. Each of you should look not only to your own interests, but also to the interests of others" (Phil. 2:3–4).

A Spirit-filled community is one where the mind of Christ is evident in the body of believers, where we find selfless servanthood. It is in this same community that we shall readily be surrounded by the fruit of the Spirit: love, joy, peace, patience, kindness, goodness, faithfulness, gentleness, and self-control (Gal. 5:22–23), all of it descriptive of "the mind of Christ." It is in such a community of joint heirs that overcomers will experience the power of God as it images the whole spectrum of His marvelous attributes. And in such a God-filled community overcomers will grow in spiritual fitness and in their ability to press on toward excellence in Christ.

Christian overcomers are persevering individuals: goal oriented, willing to work, willing to reconcile, ready to serve, and, if need be, to sacrifice. They are individuals in whom truth entered, reason prevailed, and faith triumphed. They understand what Jesus is saying, as he cries out: ". . . No one who puts his hand to the plow and looks back is fit for service in the kingdom of God" (Luke 9:62).

The words in the above quoted Scripture were addressed to an excited would-be disciple of Jesus. ". . . I will follow you. Lord; but first let me go back and say good-bye to my family" (Luke 9:61). Jesus' reply cuts to the quick. It shows that while family obligations will always be there, the call of the reign of God, as it comes through Jesus, is more urgent. "For," says Jesus, "no one who (like Lot's wife, Gen. 19:26) looks back is fit for the kingdom of God." The Spiritual fitness of Christian overcomers must be marked by a readiness to let God's rule, as Christ interprets it, be their first priority.

One of the first things that Christian overcomers must learn about the reign and realm of God is that for every gain in spiritual fitness there may also be a corresponding loss to be borne. Just as following the instructions (which were outlined earlier in this book) for physical or emotional wellness may not be possible without some pain, so—but on a much grander scale—it is in Christ's school of discipleship. The impediments to being an overcomer in Christ are difficult to overcome in isolation. It is here, once again, that the community of faith encourages, inspires, and sustains us. A community of joint and fellow heirs. A joyful community of selfless love. A community where *truth dwells, reason prevails,* and *faith triumphs.* It is in this community that the personality of Christian overcomers may be shaped or sharpened.

Christian Overcomers

All overcomers have similar characteristics, but Christian overcomers share a number of additional traits which are based on God's moral will and include love, virtue, courage against evil, obedience, forgiveness, humility, and so forth. While there are several notable differences between non-Christian and Christian overcomers, none is so great as the believer's final triumph of victory over sin, death, and the grave. Christian overcomers place a major emphasis on those traits that provide inward rest and outward victory.

Christian overcomers, like all other overcomers, share such winning personality traits as commitment, enthusiasm, and motivation. But they also have essential character traits that relate directly to the formation of a Christian mind. What is a Christian mind or personality? The Bible refers to it as a *renewed mind* (Rom. 12:2; Eph. 4:23). A mind that is updated with newly acquired Christian traits such as faith in God, forgiveness, humility, moderation, obedience, prayer, and selfless love.

When individuals consistently practice these Christian traits their overall personalities will become more and more Christlike. Before long, their daily behavior will reflect a switch from a secular to a spiritual lifestyle. It is said that they now have a transformed (or Christian) life. Such a transformed life is not the instant result of *believing* in Christ, but rather the slowly obtained result of *following* Christ. It is the outcome of *obedience* and *diligence*.

The development of a Christian personality and Christian life is a lengthy process. There is nothing quick or easy about it. But, it is, of course, quite attainable, and made a lot easier within the community of faith. The apostle Paul stresses that for the development of a Christian mind and life we must learn to concentrate on very specific character traits. He urges us to *think about* the cardinal virtues (traits) of faith, hope, love (1 Cor. 13:13), goodness, honesty, justice, loveliness, purity, and truth (Phil. 4:4–9).

Christian overcomers are challenged to seek excellence in all areas of their life. It is to be the norm, and not the exception. This excellence is to be directly evident not only in our spiritual life, but also in our cultural, emotional, mental, physical, political, social, and vocational life. Dr. Abraham Kuyper, theologian and former Prime Minister of the Netherlands (1901–1905) has said it this way: "The Holy Scripture discloses the foundation of all human life, the kind of ordinances which must govern all human existence in society and state" (Kuyper, 1933). The renewed mind (Christian personality) must affect *every* single aspect of our lives.

As Colson (1989) states, . . . if Christianity is true, then it has application for all of life, and we must seek to examine all things temporal in light of the eternal. If we concern ourselves solely with matters of faith, we talk only to ourselves."

The Final Victory

In the preface to this book we looked at some of the incredible feats performed by human beings. "Their achievements," we found, "are seemingly endless." Yet, in spite of numerous accomplishments, all too many individuals are disappointed or dissatisfied with their lives. They have failed to yield their imperfect will to the perfect will of God and do not have the joy and contentment of God's grace and peace.

Human beings can indeed do marvelous things, they can be overcomers in many areas of life, but the *final victory* is a purely spiritual one. Victory over sin, death, and the grave, come not from self-sufficiency, but are a gift from God: "For it is by grace you have been saved, through faith—and this is not from yourselves, it is the gift of God—not by works, so that no one can boast" (Eph. 2:8). There is no final triumph without the selfless love of God and the power of the resurrected Christ.

It is wonderful to be an overcomer—a determined, constructive person of sound emotions, good discernment, and healthy perseverance. But all of this has to be validated by putting our trust in Christ—we must be overcomers in Christ. "One day," writes Dr. Tony Evans, "God is going to hand out rewards to His overcomers—those Christians who weathered the storms of life and crossed the finish line victorious" (Evans, 1994). And so it is indeed, for Jesus assures all overcomers that they will "be acknowledged before God and angels . . . sit with Him on His throne . . . and be made pillars in the temple of God" (Rev. 3:5, 12, 21).

To be an overcomer involves choices. And, as the Scriptures so aptly point out, now is the time to choose and decide. Now is the time to tackle our self-defeating cognitions, to overcome our emotional struggles, to stand up against the powers of darkness, and to claim victory in Christ.

Now is the time to put the past behind us and to press on toward excellence. Now is the time to choose wisely and to love God and others. Now is the time to have a winning attitude and to fully embrace a constructive lifestyle. *Now* is the time to be an overcomer in Christ!

ENDNOTES

Chapter 2: Overcomers Stay On Course

1. Both Christian and non-Christian overcomers have winning attitudes, and both may have healthy personalities. The Christian overcomer, however, is a person who has yielded his or her own imperfect will to the perfect will of God, and, having been "saved by grace through faith," now has an even greater victory—victory over sin, death, and the grave.
2. Mainly in response to these events, on February 22, and 23, 1941, the first mass strike in wartime Holland took place in and around Amsterdam. From that time on the people lived in constant terror.
3. The contributions of the RAF and the US 8th Army Air Force flying from Britain were immense, and their losses staggering. The RAF lost 70,253 crew members, and the US 8th Army Air Force lost 44,472 crew members. In my study I have a large portrait of a young RAF pilot, Wing Commander Guy Gibson, who lost his life over Holland in 1945. He is my daily reminder of the many who have given their life for my freedom and the freedom of others.

Chapter 3: Overcomers Are Realistic Thinkers

1. In everyday-life, individuals sometimes confuse what they *assume* or *feel,* with truth. That kind of "truth" may describe subjective honesty, but not objective reality. By the same token, we must not forget that we are fallible and imperfect—we know and see in part. The importance of truth in the life of Christian believers is more fully explained in chapters 10 and 11 of this book.

Chapter 4: Overcomers Are Rational Thinkers

1. "God may on occasion ask someone to do something that seems *beyond* reason, but He will never ask us to act *irrationally.*" J. Oswald Sanders, *Every Life is a Plan of God.* (Discovery House, 1992), p. 84.

Chapter 6: Overcomers Control Their Anger

1. For a more in-depth description of personality styles, see *The Renewed Mind* (Brandt, 1999).
2. The word *embrimasthai* (basically to sniff or snort with anger) indicates an outburst of anger, and any attempt to reinterpret it in terms of an internal emotional upset caused by grief, pain, or sympathy is illegitimate" (R. Schnackenburger, *The Gospel according to St. John,* Vol. 2, 1980, p. 335); "It is beyond question that *embrimasthai* . . . implies anger" (C. K. Barrett, *The Gospel according to St. John,* 2nd edition, 1978, p. 399); "It must refer to His deep concern and indignation at the attitude of the mourners" (L. Morris, *The Gospel According to John,* 1971, p. 557).
3. Within the context of this book wholesome, constructive, and solution-focused self-talk are used synonymously. All three are based on realism, reason, and optimism, or truth, reason, and faith.
4. The contents of this chapter on anger go hand-in-hand with the contents of Chapter 9 (*Overcomers Lead Happier Lives*).

Chapter 7: Overcomers Manage Their Anxieties

1. The mitral valve is one of four valves of the heart and allows blood to flow from the left atrium to the left ventricle while preventing any back-flow. In MVP this process is somewhat flawed. The prolapse (sinking down) of the valve allows a slight back–flow of blood. The latter is heard by a physician as a so-called "click-murmur." By itself, MVP is usually regarded as a harmless condition.
2. Breathing incorrectly makes a person more vulnerable to anxiety problems, but anxiety itself may also lead to improper breathing. Either "breath-holding" or, more likely, "hyperventilation" is the result. In hyperventilation there is sharp and rapid breathing, which leads to changes in body chemistry (too much carbon dioxide is expelled), with such symptoms as anxiety; dizziness; blurred vision; panic attacks; palpitations; numbness or tingling in hands or feet; chest, muscle, or joint pain; breathlessness; and other symptoms. It is also a good idea to consume some extra calcium, as this is low at times in anxious and depressed persons. Hyperventilation tends to lower blood calcium levels as well. Healthy calcium-rich juice drinks can be made by juicing seven ounces of carrots, four ounces of apples, and three ounces of

spinach, *or* by juicing six carrots, four kale leaves, four sprigs of parsley, and half of an apple. Try it, you will like it!

3. J. Maarse, *Facetten van Zelfbeheersing*, U.M. West Friesland, Hoorn, Netherlands, 1962, p. 208.

4. If only we would fully grasp this truth, we might stop judging people, stop meddling and prying into their private lives, stop making odious comparisons, and start to have more kindness, patience, mercy, and humility. *We could be cured of the ignorance of our arrogance.* We could come to understand that "a man's ways seem right to him . . ." (Prov. 21:2), yet perhaps perceived differently by someone else; that we see dimly and incompletely, and know only partially (1 Cor. 13:12), but that love (acceptance, respect, care, understanding) is to be the abiding guide in our dealings with others (1 Cor. 13:13).

5. The contents of this chapter on anxiety go hand-in-hand with the contents of Chapter 9 (*Overcomers Lead Happier Lives*).

Chapter 8: Overcomers Defeat Their Depressions

1. The *hypothalamus* actually is one of two "switchboards" in the brain. It receives messages *directly* from the thalamus (which consists of two large oval shaped masses of gray matter which are found deep in the cerebral hemispheres, and which relay sensory impulses to and from the cerebral cortex), and *indirectly* from the thalamus (via the limbic system, whose structures–the *hippocampus, amygdala,* and *gyrus fornicatus*–lie close to the edge (limbus) of the cerebral hemisphere midline. The limbic system, which I frequently refer to as the "feeling portion" of the brain, is sometimes "conveniently" assumed to include the hypothalamus. The latter influences both the sympathetic branch of the autonomic nervous system and (via the pituitary gland) the endocrine system. The *thalamus* is perhaps best seen as the "main switchboard." When it receives sensory impulses it not only notifies the *hippocampus* (emotional memories) and *amygdala* (emotional reactions), but also the frontal and pre-frontal cortex where sensory input is sorted out and behavioral strategies are developed. The cortex, in turn, sends messages to the *amygdala* (in addition to those received from the hippocampus). For practical purposes—to make it easier to understand that our emotional responses are the result of our apperceptions—it is helpful to many people to simply think of the brain in terms of a thinking portion (cortex) and feeling portion (limbic system). The more we think right, the more we feel right (cf, Endnotes 1, 2, Chapter 9).

2. One physician, for example, wrote: "Your insights about stress levels and its interrelationship with the disease process called depression rings

loud and true. Neuronal pathway dysfunction and misinterpretation of external stimuli are a hallmark of this disorder. The emotional reeducation process of learning to choose wise and healthy goals, make life and health-preserving decisions, and choosing conflict-reducing behaviors, fits like hand and glove with the scientific understanding of brain chemistry and psychodynamics. Thoughts, beliefs, attitudes, and opinions can change for the better through the tandem efforts of wise counsel and good medicine. I have witnessed this several hundred times in patients I have treated with confidence and conviction this last year. My blueprint for therapy has been formulated by what you have written and shared with me over this last year."

3. "Depressie: Een Zichtbare Hersenafwijking: *De Telegraaf*, Amsterdam, The Netherlands, June 11, 1994.

4. Primary Care Update: Better Treatments for Depression, CME, Inc., April 1995, Santa Anna, CA, 92705-9965.

5. Specifically with shortages of certain vitamins, minerals, and amino acids.

6. Spiritual regeneration (cf. John 3:3; Titus 2:11–14) should, of course, be sought for its own sake, not merely as an element in the treatment of depression. Nevertheless it is listed here because where a given depression has a spiritual root it can only be relieved by a spiritual remedy.

7. On the glycemic index, fructose is virtually at the bottom, with a measly 20–29%, compared to sucrose with 50–59%, honey with 80–89%, and glucose with 100%.

8. Ater Jenkins, D.J.A., Lente Carbohydrate: A Newer Approach to the Dietary Management of Diabetes, *Diabetes Care* 5:631–641, 1982.

Chapter 9: Overcomers Lead Happier Lives

1. The *amygdala*—the storehouse of our emotional reactions and responses is an almond-shaped mass of gray matter on the bottom sides of the cerebrum. The *hippocampus*—the storehouse of our emotional memories—lies close to the amygdala and plays an important role in the regulation of our emotions. The *hypothalamus*—which is closely connected to the limbic system—controls the endocrine system and sympathetic branch of the autonomic nervous system, and has numerous functions, including the regulation of moods, hunger, thirst, and body temperature. It is directly influenced by the *thalamus*–one of two oval-shaped masses of gray matter that lie deeply in the cerebral hemispheres—which serves as a kind of sensory impulse "switchboard" for our cerebral cortex.

2. In this chapter I emphasize that we must think right if we want to feel right. While this is true, we must not forget that this requires a healthy brain. For example, we must be able to learn and remember new information. And for that we need, among other things, a well-functioning *hippocampus*. The latter, however, as well as other parts of the neonatal brain, can be damaged by a number of events. One such event is the consumption of alcohol during pregnancy. It is well-known that heavy consumption of alcohol during pregnancy may lead to neurological and other problems known as fetal alcohol syndrome (FAS) in a mother's offspring. But, there are warnings that even *moderate consumption of alcohol* during pregnancy may have long-term negative effects in such areas as learning and memory. Sutherland, McDonald, and Savage (1997) report that ". . . prenatal exposure to moderate ethanol levels can produce a long-lasting deficit in synaptic enhancement in a neural pathway believed to be critical in certain forms of learning and memory." For more information on the importance of a healthy body for a healthy mind, and vice-versa, see *The Renewed Mind* (Brandt, 1999), and the last section of this chapter.
3. Events in this section refer to perceptions, self-talk and emotions.
4. Many of the thinking errors discussed in this section were first identified by Dr. Aaron Beck and his associates. See Aaron T. Beck, Thinking and Depression: Idiosyncratic Content and Cognitive Distortions, *Archives of General Psychiatry 10,* 561–571, 1963.
5. Vegetarian diets and lifestyles have been lauded as *the key* to optimum wellness by many health professionals over the past century, and even long before that. Worldwide reports show that vegetarianism may well provide the optimum diet for most individuals. Nevertheless, there are also reports that some individuals seem to do just fine on a variety of other diets, and that some vegetarians apparently are no healthier than meat eaters. A vegetarian diet, in my opinion, is only one factor in any health and longevity equation. I believe that a healthy diet is the most important aspect of a healthy lifestyle, but that other supremely important factors are also at play in those who enjoy robust health and long lives. First and foremost, I think, is *attitude.* Those who have a winning and happy predisposition ("death and life are in the power of the tongue") are way ahead of the power-curve. Next I am thinking about the importance of *exercise.* It is a major force in both the prevention and healing of just about any illness. And there are other obvious factors such as *freedom from addictive substances, breathing healthy air,* and *consuming organic foods* (free from pesticides, herbicides, and so forth). Abstaining from animal products, but living a life of pessimism, doubt,

fear, and worry and fortifying ourselves with daily doses of refined carbohydrates (especially candy and other sugar-laden products, e.g. certain breakfast cereals) or consuming tap water, so-called "soft" drinks, and other unhealthy products, is not going to offset the benefits gained by not eating animal products. The secret to good health and a long and happy life is found in a *healthy lifestyle*—spirit, mind, and body—the overcomer's lifestyle!

Chapter 10:Overcomers Are Alert Survivors in an Age of Folly

1. John Milton, *Paradise Lost*, I, 47, 60, 263, 258–9.
2. Georges Bernanos, *The Diary of a Country Priest*, 81.
3. Charles Colson, "The Year of the Neopagan," in *Christianity Today*, March 6, 1995, 88.
4. Incest is a universal problem. While rejected and considered taboo, we find that incest and child abuse have been around since the dawn of culture. In America this problem although horrendous is believed to be less common than in many other cultures. And certainly it is far less common among Christians than those of some other persuasions. Nevertheless, even one case of child abuse is one too many. It is despicable, and Christians must be united in full condemnation of it.
5. Both predators and cultic leaders ultimately seek complete control over others. They will skillfully, e.g. through ingratiation, seek to subtly influence those they have targeted. After getting an emotional foothold, e.g. through getting "confessions," or obtaining "secrets," they will next instill some form of fear in their victims, e.g. a fear about other people, other religious groups, and so forth. Instilling paranoid delusions in others is one of their favorite techniques! Finally, they will resort to any persuasive means to keep tight control over their victims. This process is usually so insidious that the victims are completely unaware that they are being trapped by a predator.

Chapter 11:   Overcomers Resist Follies of All Kinds

1. Langone (1988) lists the following suggestibility factors: "dependency, desire for spiritual meaning, gullibility, ignorance of the ways in which groups can manipulate individuals, low tolerance for ambiguity, significant stress, susceptibility to trance-like states, naive idealism, unassertiveness."
2. Farewell sermon at the Domkerk at Utrecht, Holland, 31 July 1870 (James D. Bratt, Ed., *Abraham Kuyper, A Centennial Reader,* Eerdmans, 1998).
3. In psychotherapy the term "narcissism" refers to patterns of grandiosity, need for admiration, and lack of true empathy.

4. Langone (1988) states that the New Age movement's "fundamental tenet is that men are blind to the fact that they are all one, that they are all God, that they are all capable of developing superhuman capacities."

5. John Cassian, Conferences II, 2, in *Classics of Western Spirituality*, Paulist Press, 61–62, 1985.

6. Joseph Piper, quoted in Lewis B. Smedes, *A Pretty Good Person*, Harper & Row, 1990, 143.

7. God is love. And thus the "spirit of love" is the spirit of God. It is not a matter of words, slogans, or worse, a cloak of self-righteousness about who we are. All too many speak of charity or love, but do the exact opposite, and thus bring discredit to the cause of Christ. We cannot have any part of the spirit of love, unless we "do" what that spirit calls for. We need to imitate the selfless love of God, by ministering to those who cannot, will not, and in any case are not required, to do anything at all for us. God's spirit of love gave His Son to us who were lost and needy. What do we give to our brethren who are lost and needy?

Chapter 12: Overcomers Press On Toward Excellence

1. For example, in spite of numerous programs, and the spending of millions of dollars, the use of drugs, according to the U.S. Department of Health and Human Services, among America's teenagers went up by nearly 80% between 1992 and 1995,. A continued decline in teaching and modeling values at home, school, and elsewhere, as well as lack of boundaries, structure, and good example by society at large, and leadership in particular, are key issues here.

2. "Christianity could not survive without the ongoing community through which it is proclaimed, practiced (to a greater or lesser degree), and propagated. It is not isolated individuals who accomplish this; it is the fellowship of believers. Wherever the name of Christ is known and acknowledged today, it is because the Church has been there" (Robert McAfee Brown, *The Bible Speaks to You* [Philadelphia: Westminster Press, 1955], p. 202).

3. In response to relativism we do well to recognize that our thoughts, beliefs, and attitudes can only be as objective as the extent of our genetic endowment, imperfect knowledge, and limited experiences in a very subjective world allow. Subjective to the extent that little of the world is known to even the most scholarly and best informed scientists. We are fallible human beings; we are not God!

4. Henry H. Halley, in his discussion of the Garden of Eden, writes that the tree of life ". . . may have been an actual food of immortality, indicating that immortality is dependent on something outside of ourselves. This Tree will again be accessible to those who have washed their robes in the blood of the Lamb (Rev. 2:7; 22:2, 14)." *Halley's Bible Handbook*, Regency Reference Library, Zondervan Publishing House, Grand Rapids, 1965.

5. "Christians find that their ethical concerns are strengthened by their corporate life together. As Christians do things together, they not only strengthen and undergird one another, but they also find that God himself strengthens and undergirds what they do" (Robert McAfee Brown, 1995, p. 202).

References

Atkins, Frederick A. Ed. (1900). *The Young Man*. London: Horace Marshall and Son, Vol. XIV.

Barrett, C. K. (1955). *The Gospel According to St. John*. London, S.P.C.K.

Baer, Randall N. (1989). *Inside the New Age Nightmare*. Lafayette, LA: Huntington House, Inc.

Bernanos, Georges. (1948). *The Diary of a Country Priest*. New York: The Macmillan Company.

Brandt, Frans M. J. (1977). *A Rational Self-Counseling Primer*. Kelsale Court, Saxmundham, Suffolk, England: Institute for Rational Therapy.

Brandt, Frans M. J. (1979). *A Guide to Rational Weight Control*. Kelsale Court, Saxmundham, Suffolk, England: Institute for Rational Therapy.

Brandt, Frans M. J. (1984). *The Way to Wholeness*. Westchester, IL: Crossway Books.

Brandt, Frans M. J. (1988). *Victory Over Depression*. Grand Rapids: Baker Book House.

Brandt, Frans M. J. (1992). *The Classification, Diagnosis, and Treatment of Personality Disorders*. Paper presented to the National Council of Psychotherapists, Royal Society of Medicine, London, England.

Brandt, Frans M. J. (1998). *Personality and Love*. East Tawas, MI: Brandt Human Development Consulting.

Brandt, Frans M. J. (1999). *The Renewed Mind*. Enumclaw, WA: WinePress Publishing.

Bratt, James D. Ed. (1998). *Abraham Kuyper: A Centennial Reader*. Grand Rapids, MI: William B. Eerdmans Publishing Company.

Bridges, Jerry. (1988). *Trusting God*. Colorado Springs: NavPress.

Bridges, Jerry. (1994). *The Discipline of Grace*. Colorado Springs: NavPress.

Brown, Robert McAfee. (1955). *The Bible Speaks to You*. Philadelphia, PA: The Westminster Press.

Buechner, Frederick. (1969). *The Hungering Dark*. New York: Seabury Press.

Burton, Robert. (1845). *The Anatomy of Melancholy*. London: Thomas Tegg.

Carlson, Carole C. (1983). *Corrie ten Boom: Her Life, Her Faith*. Old Tappan, NJ: Fleming H. Revell Company.

Cassian, John. (1985). Conferences II, 2. *Classics of Western Spirituality*. New York: Paulist Press, 61–62.

Chambers, Oswald. (1985). *The Love of God*. Grand Rapids: Discovery House.

Chambers, Oswald. (1989). *The Best From All His Books, II*. Nashville: Oliver Nelson Books, Thomas Nelson, Inc.

Chambers, Oswald. (1993). *So Send I You/Workmen of God*. Grand Rapids: Discovery House.

Chambers, Oswald. (1995). *Christian Disciplines*. Grand Rapids: Discovery House.

Colson, Charles. (1989). *Against the Night*. Ann Arbor, MI: Servant Publications.

Colson, Charles. (March 6, 1995). "The Year of the Neopagan." *Christianity Today*.

Costello, Charles C. (1996). *Personality Characteristics of the Personality Disordered*. New York: John Wiley & Sons, Inc.

Depressie: Een Zichtbare Hersenafwijking. (June 11, 1994). *De Telegraaf*. Amsterdam, The Netherlands.

Derksen, Jan. (1995). *Personality Disorders*. Chister, England: John Wiley & Sons, Ltd.

Diagnostic and Statistical Manual of Mental Disorders, DSM-IV. (1994). Washington: American Psychiatric Association.

Disciple's Study Bible: New International Version. (1988). Nashville: Holman Bible Publishers.

Dobson, James C. (1991). *Straight Talk*. Dallas: Word Publishing.

Dobson, James C. (1994). *Love for a Lifetime*. Sisters, OR: Multnomah Books.

Dowley, Tim, Ed. (1990). *The History of Christianity*. Batavia, IL: Lion Publishing.

Encyclopedia of Biblical and Christian Ethics. (1987). Nashville: Thomas Nelson Publishers.

Eareckson, Joni. (1976). *Joni*. Minneapolis: World Wide Publications.

Evans, Toni. (1994). *A Guide to Spiritual Success*. Nashville: Thomas Nelson Publishing.

Freeman, Hobart E. (1969). *Angels of Light?* Plainfield, NJ: Logos International.

Friedman, Howard S. (1990). *Personality and Disease*. New York: John Wiley and Sons, Inc.

Ganong, W. F., M. F. Dallman, and J. L. Roberts. (1987). *The Hypothalamic-Pituitary Adrenal Axis Revisited*. New York: The New York Academy of Sciences.

Garety, Phillippa A., and David R. Hemsley. (1997). *Delusions*. Hove, East Sussex, England: Psychology Press Ltd.

Girzone, Joseph F. (1995). *Joshua*. New York: Simon & Schuster.

Goleman, Daniel. (1995). *Emotional Intelligence*. New York: Bantam Books.

Gordon, S. D. (1903). *Quiet Talks on Power*. New York: Grosset and Dunlap.

Graham, Billy. (1978). *The Holy Spirit*. Waco, TX: Word Books.

Groothuis, Douglas R. (1986). *Unmasking the New Age*. Downers Grove, IL: InterVarsity Press.

Gruss, Edmond C. (1973). *What About the Quija Board?* Chicago: Moody Press.

Gruss, Edmund C. (1974). *Cults and the Occult*. Nutley, N.J.: Presbyterian and Reformed Publishing Co.

Halley, Henry H. (1965). *Halley's Bible Handbook*. Grand Rapids: Zondervan Publishing House.

Harvey, Willard F. (1986). *His Needs, Her Needs*. New York: Fleming H. Revell Company.

Hybels, Bill. (1990). *Honest to God?* Grand Rapids: Zondervan Publishing House.

Jenkins, D. J. A. Lente Carbohydrate: A Newer Approach to Dietary Management of Diabetes. (1982). *Diabetes Care* 5:631—641.

Johnson, Wendell. (1946). *People in Quandaries*. New York: Harper & Brothers.

Johnston, Kirk J. (1994). *When Counseling is Not Enough*. Grand Rapids: Discovery House.

Jones, Peter. (1997). *Spirit Wars*. Mukilteo, WA: WinePress.

Keller, Helen. (1940). *Let Us Have Faith*. New York, Double Day, Doran & Co., Inc.

Keller, Helen. (1954). *The Story of My Life*. Garden City, NY: Doubleday & Company, Inc.

Keller, W. Philip. (1992). *Serenity*. Grand Rapids: Baker Book House.

Kirk, Kenneth E. (1961). *Some Principles of Moral Theology*. London: Longmans, Green and Co., Ltd..

Koocher, Gerald P., John C. Norcross, and Sam S. Hill III, Eds. (1998). *Psychologist's Desk Reference*. New York: Oxford University Press.

Kuyper, Abraham. (1931). *Lectures on Calvinism*. Eerdmans Publishing Company.

Langone, Michael. (1988). *Cults: Questions and Answers*. Bonita Springs, FL: American Family Foundation.

Langone, Michael. (1993). *Recovery from Cults*. New York: W. W. Norton & Company.

Lasch, Christopher. (1979). *The Culture of Narcissism*. New York: W. W. Norton & Company, Inc.

Lash, Joseph P. (1980). *Helen and Teacher*. New York: Delacorte Press/ Seymour Lawrence.

Lewis, C. S. (1944). *The Screwtape Letters*. New York: MacMillan Co.

Lewis, C. S. (1949). *The Weight of Glory and Other Addresses*. New York: MacMillan Co.

Liebman, Joshua Loth. (1946). *Peace of Mind*. New York: Simon and Schuster.

Luther, Martin. Lectures on Romans. (1961). *Library of Christian Classics*. Philadelphia: Westminster Press.

Maarse, J. (1955). *Toorn, Haat en Zelfbeheersing*. Hoorn, The Netherlands: U.M. West Friesland.

Maarse, J. (1962). *Facetten van Zelfbeheersing*. Hoorn, The Netherlands: U.M. West Friesland.

Martin, Walter, (1985). *The Kingdom of the Cults*. Minneapolis: Bethany House Publishers.

Millon, Theodore. (1996). *Disorders of Personality, DSM-IV and Beyond*. New York: John Wiley Sons, Inc.

Millon, Theodore. (1996). *Personality and Psychopathology: Building a Clinical Science*. New York: John Wiley & Sons, Inc.

Milton, John. (1966). *Paradise Lost*. London and New York: Cassell, Petter, and Galpin.

Montapert, Alfred A. (1964). *Distilled Wisdom*. Englewood Cliffs, NJ: Prentice-Hall, Inc.

Morris, L. (1971). *The Gospel According to John*. Grand Rapids: Eerdmans Publishing Company.

Murphy, Daniel. (1995). *Comenius*. Dublin: Irish Academic press.

Nataf, Andre. (1991). *The Occult*. Edinburgh; New York: Chambers.

New Marked Reference Bible, Being the King James Authorized Version of the Old and New Testaments. (1983). Grand Rapids: Zondervan Bible Publishers,

Osborn, Lawrence, (1992). *Angels of Light*. London: Daybreak. Darton, Longman and Todd Ltd.

Ouweneel, W. J. (1978). *Het Domein van de Slang*. Amsterdam, The Netherlands: Buijten en Schipperheijn.

Overduin, J. (1967). *Worden Als Een Man*. Wageningen, The Netherlands: N.V. Gebr. Zomer & Keunings Uitgeversmaatschappij,

Packer, J. I. (1993). *Knowing God.* Downers Grove, IL: InterVarsity Press.

Peterson, Eugene H. (1994). *The Message Psalms.* Colorado Springs: NavPress

Piper, John. (1986). *Desiring God.* Sisters, OR: Multnomah Press.

Plantinga, Cornelius, Jr. (1995). *Not the Way It's Supposed to Be: A Breviary of Sin.* Grand Rapids: Eerdmans Publishing Company.

Poley, Hans. (1993). *Return to the Hiding Place.* Elgin, IL: Chariot Family Publishing.

Primary Care Update: Better Treatment for Depression. (April 1995). *CME, Inc.* Santa Ana, CA.

Rachman, S. (1968). *Phobias.* Springfield, IL: Charles C. Thomas.

Robinson, Haddon W. (1991). *What Jesus Said About Successful Living.* Grand Rapids: Discovery House.

Roland, Per E. (1993). *Brain Activation.* New York: Wiley-Liss, Inc.

Sheen, Fulton J. (1954). *Way to Happiness.* Garden City, NY: Garden City Books.

Singer, Margaret Thaler. (1995). *Cults in Our Midst.* San Francisco: Jossey-Bass Publishers.

Smedes, Lewis B. (1990). *A Pretty Good Person.* San Francisco: Harper and Row.

Schnackenburger, R. (1980–1982). *The Gospel According to St. John.* New York: Seabury Press.

Solomon, Marion F. (1989). *Narcissism and Intimacy.* New York: W. W. Norton & Co., Inc.

Spurgeon, Charles. (1993). *The Power of Prayer in a Believer's Life.* Lynnwood, WA: Emerald Books.

Stearns, Frederic R. (1972). *Anger: Psychology, Physiology, Pathology.* Springfield, IL: Charles C. Thomas.

Stone, Michael H. (1993). *Abnormalities of Personality.* New York: W. W. Norton & Company.

Stott, John R. W. (1981). *Our Guilty Silence.* Grand Rapids: Eerdmans Publishing Company.

Stott, John R.W. (1991). *You Can Trust the Bible.* Grand Rapids: Discovery House.

Sugarman, Shirley. (1976). *Sin and Madness. Studies in Narcissism.* Philadelphia: Westminster Press.

Sutherland, Robert J., Robert J McDonald, and Daniel D. Savage. Prenatal Exposure to Moderate Levels of Ethanol Can Have Long-Lasting Effects on Hippocampus Synaptic Plasticity in Adult Offspring. (1997). *Hippocampus* 7:232–238.

Sutherland, Stuart. (1996). *The International Dictionary of Psychology.* 2nd ed. New York: Crossroad.

Tannen, Deborah. (1990). *You Just Don't Understand.* New York: Ballantine Books.

Tannen, Deborah. (1994). *Talking from 9 to 5.* New York: William Morrow and Company, Inc.

Ten Boom, Corrie. (1953). *Amazing Love.* London: Christian Literature Crusade.

Ten Boom, Corrie. (1963). *Defeated Enemies.* Fort Washington, PA: Christian Literature Crusade.

Ten Boom, Corrie. (1976). *In My Father's House.* Old Tappan, NJ: Fleming H. Revell Co.

Ten Boom, Corrie, and Jamie Buckingham. (1974). *Tramp for the Lord.* Old Tappan NJ: Fleming H. Revell Company.

The Amplified Bible. (1987). Grand Rapids: Zondervan Bible Publishers.

Tuckman, Barbara. (1984). *The March of Folly.* New York: Knopf. Distributed by Random House.

Van der Hoop, J.H. (1933). *Zielkunde en de Zin Van Ons Leven.* Amsterdam: H. J. Paris.

Watts, A. E. (1954). *Ovid, Metamorphoses, III.* Berkeley, CA: University of California Press.

Way, Lewis. (1948). *Man's Quest for Significance.* London: George Allen & Unwin, Ltd.

Wellek, Albert. (1959). *Die Polarität Im Aufbau Des Charakters.* Bern: Francke Verlag.

Wijngaarden, H. R. (1959). *Gesprekken Met U Zelf.* Utrecht: Netherlands: Erven J. Bijleveld.

SUBJECT INDEX

Age of Folly, xviii, 131–165
Allness thinking, 107, 108
Amygdala, 113, 114, 184
Anger, 61–75
  adolescents and, 63
  adults and, 63
  aggressive, 63–65, 67–69,
    171–172
  antisocial personality and, 63
  assertive, 65, 66
  blood glucose levels and, 70
  borderline personalities and, 63
  children and, 63
  choice and, 68
  constrained, 63
  cultural aspects of, 62, 63
  definition of, 62
  destructive, 67, 69
  developmental aspects of, 62, 63
  depression and, 65, 67
  diet and, 65, 70, 123–125, 185,
    186
  dual nature of, 69
  emotional aspects of, 64–66
  emotional disorders and, 63
  emotional re-education for, 70–74,
    111–125
  exercise and, 184
  God and, 64, 66, 74
  illness and, 65, 68, 70
  infants and, 63
  irrational, 65
  Jesus and, 67
  loss and, 65
  medications and, 71
  men and, 63
  narcissistic personality and, 63
  negativistic personality and, 63, 64
  normal, 61, 62, 64–67
  Old Testament and, 66
  overcoming, 69–75, 111–128
  paranoid personality and, 63
  personality aspects of, 63, 64
  physical aspects of, 67–69, 70, 71
  physical intervention for, 70, 71,
    125–128
  positive, 66
  psychological intervention for, 71,
    74
  rage and, 64

rational, 65, 66
realistic, 66
righteous, 65, 66, 67
self-talk and, 66, 72–74, 98, 115, 116
spiritual aspects of, 66, 67, 70
spiritual intervention for, 74, 75
stress and, 64, 67
substance withdrawal and, 70
supressed, 68
survival and, 68
understanding, 62–69
women and, 63, 67
Anxiety, 77–94
    allergic reactions and, 79
    arbitrary inferences and, 78
    blood glucose levels and, 80
    breathing and, 88, 89
    caffeine and, 79, 80
    catastrophizing and, 78
    definition of, 77
    diet and, 79, 87, 88, 123–125, 185, 186
    disorders, 77, 82–84
    emotional aspects of, 78, 79, 82–84
    emotional re-education for, 89, 111–125
    endocrine disorders and, 79
    fear and, 78
    God and, 90–94
    inflammatory disease and, 79
    Jesus and, 90–94
    loss and, 85
    medications and, 86
    Mitral Valve Prolapse and, 80
    neurological problems and, 79
    nutritional aspects of, 80
    overcoming, 86–94, 111–128
    overgeneralization and, 79
    physical antidotes for, 86–89

physical aspects of, 79, 80, 82, 83, 87, 88
    psychological intervention for, 89
    self-talk and, 89, 114, 116–118
    sources versus causes of, 80, 81
    spiritual aspects of, 84–86
    spiritual intervention for, 90–94
    stress and, 78, 81, 82, 87
    systemic disorders and, 79
    thinking errors and, 78, 79, 84, 89
    toxic conditions and, 79
    understanding, 77–86
Arbitrary inferences, 78, 121
Attitudes, xvi–xviii
    definition of, 22, 29, 92, 112
    power of, 22–27

Biased attribution, 121
Biochemical stress, 103
Bipolar Disorders, 104
Blood glucose levels,
    food and, 106, 107

Catastrophizing, 78, 79, 121
Cheerfulness, 53, 54
Cognitive distortions. *See* Errors in thinking.
Compulsions,
    definition of, 83, 146
Consensus misattribution, 121
Cultism, 145–147
Cult leaders,
    characteristics of, 146, 147
Cults, 139, 140, 145, 147
    characteristics of, 140
    Christian, 146

Depression, 95–110
    adrenal cortex and, 96
    adrenal medulla and, 96

biochemical aspects of, 96, 97, 101–103
causes of, 95–104
Christians and, 108–110
definition of, 95
diet and, 103, 105–107, 123–125, 184, 185
God and, 99, 101, 108–110
loss and, 98
medications for, 104, 105
overcoming, 104–110, 111–128
physical restoration for, 104–107
physical sources of, 95–97, 100
psychological sources of, 98, 100, 101
root sources of, 100, 101
self-talk and, 98, 99, 107, 108, 114–116, 118, 119
spiritual sources of, 99–100, 101
stress and, 95–97
sugar sensitivity and, 105–107
thyroid dysfunction and, 97
understanding, 95–104
Depressive illness, 100
Dichotomous thinking, 121
Discernment, 156–165
mental, 151–159
spiritual, 161–163
Dissonance,
mental–emotional, 73
Domination, 142, 146, 153, 162, 173, 185, 186

Emotionalism, 147, 148
Emotional problems,
physical roots of, 123–128
Emotional reasoning, 121
Emotional reeducation, 72–74, 107
Emotions,
amygdala and, 114, 184
anatomy of, 111–120

diet and, 123–125
hippocampus and, 114, 184
hypothalamus and, 102
neocortex and, 112, 113
normal versus problematic, 61, 62
perceptions and, 111–120
self-talk and, 114–120
Errors in thinking, 120–122
Evil, 156, 172–174
Evil doers, 163

Factual thinking. See Realistic thinking.
Faith, xv, 57, 58
Fallibility, human, 73, 171
False prophets, 161–163, 171
characteristics of, 162, 163
False teachers, 161–163
characteristics of, 162, 163
Fanaticism, 148, 150
Fatalism, 149, 150
Feelings,
thinking and, 61, 74, 78, 79, 98, 184
Follies,
blindness of, 135
common, 145, 146
discernment versus, 158, 159
human history of, 136–138
Fortune telling, 122

Generalized Anxiety Disorder, 82
Genesis diet, 123, 124, 185, 186
Glycemic index, 106, 107
God-confusion, 85, 109
God-filled community, the 174–176
Godless community, the 173, 174
God-neglect, 85, 110
God-void, 85, 109, 111
Happiness, requirements for, 111

Health,
  lifestyle and, 49, 123–128, 184–185
Hedonism, 150, 151
Hippocampus, 103, 114, 184
Holy Spirit, 58, 93, 94
Humanism, 151
Hypothalamus, 97, 98, 100, 103, 112, 184

Illness, lifestyle and, 123–128, 184, 185
Immorality, 140–143, 186, 187
Insight,
  emotional, 73
  intellectual, 72
Intimidation, 142, 146 153, 162, 173, 185, 186

Justification, 58

Kingdom of God, 91–93

Limbic system, 112, 113
Love, 24, 85, 163, 164, 175, 179, 187

Magnification, 122
Manipulation, 142, 146, 153, 162, 173, 185, 186
Mental health,
  nutrition and, 123–128, 185, 186
Mental practice, 114, 123
  examples of, 115–120
Mind reading, 122
Minimization, 122

Narcissism, 63, 152, 153, 173
Negative memory bias, 122
New Age, 138, 139, 186
Nutrition,

mental health and, 123–128, 184, 185

Obsessive Compulsive Disorder, 83
Obsessions,
  definition of, 83
Occultism, 56, 57
Overcomers, xv–xviii, 22–27, 45, 53, 93, 169–179
  definition of, 44, 178
Overgeneralization, 79, 122

Panic Disorder, 82
Perceptions, 111, 112, 115–119
  definition of , 102
Personality,
  Christian, 176–178
  healthy, xviii, 169
  unhealthy, 63, 64
Phobic Disorder, 82, 83
Physical health,
  nutrition and, 123–125, 185, 186
Positive thinking, 53–58, 171
  cheerfulness and, 53, 54
  confidence and, 54–56
  faith and, 57, 58
  optimism and, 56, 57
Posttraumatic Stress Disorder, 83, 84
Prayer, 91–94
Predators, 140–143, 172, 186, 187
Pride,
  lineage of, 133–135
Rational thinking, xv, 47–51
  goal achieving and, 49, 50
  Jesus and, 44
  life-saving nature of, 48, 49
  sound decisions and, 47, 48
Realistic thinking, 43–46
  Christians and, 43–46
  factual nature of, 43, 44
  Jesus and, 44

truth and, 45, 46
Reason. *See* Rational thinking.
Religion, false, 161–163
Renewed mind, 175

Sanctification, 58
Salvation, 26, 58, 74, 85, 109, 110,
   174, 178
Satan, 133–135
Self-talk, 114–120
   examples of, 115–120
   power of, 74, 114
   scripts, 115–120
   verification of, 114, 157
Sound decision making,
   formula for, 114, 157
Sources verses causes, 74, 80, 81, 88,
   102
Spiritual discernment 160–165

Thoughts,
   feelings and, 112, 113
   perceptions and, 112
   power of, 21, 22, 112–120

Wholesome self-talk, 114–122, 125
   formula for, 114, 157; *See also* Constructive thinking; Self-talk.
Wisdom, 131–133, 147, 148
   definition of, 132

To order additional copies of

THE CONSISTENT
OVERCOMER

Call (800)917-BOOK

or send $14.95 plus $3.95 shipping and handling to

Books Etc.
P.O. Box 4888
Seattle, WA 98104